YOUR
HOROSCOPE

2009

AQUARIUS

YOUR PERSONAL HOROSCOPE 2009

AQUARIUS

21st January–19th February

igloo

igloo

This edition published by Igloo Books Ltd,
Cottage Farm, Sywell, Northants NN6 0BJ
www.igloo-books.com

Produced for Igloo Books by W. Foulsham & Co. Ltd,
The Publishing House, Bennetts Close, Cippenham,
Slough, Berkshire SL1 5AP, England

ISBN: 978-1-84817-054-4

This is an abridged version of material
originally published in *Old Moore's Horoscope
and Astral Diary*.

Printed and manufactured in China

CONTENTS

INTRODUCTION

Your Personal Horoscopes have been specifically created to allow you to get the most from astrological patterns and the way they have a bearing on not only your zodiac sign, but nuances within it. Using the diary section of the book you can read about the influences and possibilities of each and every day of the year. It will be possible for you to see when you are likely to be cheerful and happy or those times when your nature is in retreat and you will be more circumspect. The diary will help to give you a feel for the specific 'cycles' of astrology and the way they can subtly change your day-to-day life. For example, when you see the sign ☿, this means that the planet Mercury is retrograde at that time. Retrograde means it appears to be running backwards through the zodiac. Such a happening has a significant effect on communication skills, but this is only one small aspect of how the Personal Horoscope can help you.

With Your Personal Horoscope the story doesn't end with the diary pages. It includes simple ways for you to work out the zodiac sign the Moon occupied at the time of your birth, and what this means for your personality. In addition, if you know the time of day you were born, it is possible to discover your Ascendant, yet another important guide to your personal make-up and potential.

Many readers are interested in relationships and in knowing how well they get on with people of other astrological signs. You might also be interested in the way you appear to very different sorts of individuals. If you are such a person, the section on Venus will be of particular interest. Despite the rapidly changing position of this planet, you can work out your Venus sign, and learn what bearing it will have on your life.

Using Your Personal Horoscope you can travel on one of the most fascinating and rewarding journeys that anyone can take – the journey to a better realisation of self.

THE ESSENCE
OF AQUARIUS

Exploring the Personality of
Aquarius the Water Carrier
(21ST JANUARY– 19TH FEBRUARY)

What's in a sign?

Oh, what a wonderful person you can be! Despite a number of contradictions and one of the most complicated natures to be found anywhere in the zodiac, you certainly know how to make friends and influence people. Your ruling planet is Uranus, one of the more recently discovered members of the solar system's family. It rules modern communications, such as radio and television, and also has a response to the recent discoveries of science. It is within the world of 'the modern' that you reside and you have little or no difficulty keeping up with the ever-increasing pace of life.

People naturally like you and it's not surprising. You are open, liberal, and rarely judgmental, and you are often surrounded by deeply original and even eccentric types. Life to you is a storybook full of fascinating tales. Aquarians amass information 'on the hoof' and very little passes you by. Understanding what makes others tick is meat and drink to you and proves to be a source of endless joy. Unlike the other Air signs of Gemini and Libra, you are able to spend long hours on your own if necessary and always keep your mind active.

Aquarians have great creative potential; they are refined, often extremely well educated and they remain totally classless. This makes it easy for you to get on with just about any sort of person and also explains your general success in the material world. You are fascinating, original, thought-provoking and even quite deep on occasions. Matters that take months for others to synthesise, you can absorb in minutes. It is clear to everyone that you are one of life's natural leaders, but when you head any organisation you do so by co-operation and example because you are not in the least authoritarian.

In love you can be ardent and sincere – for a while at least. You need to be loved and it's true that deeply personal relationships can be a problem to you if they are not supplying what is most important to you. Few people know the real you, because your nature exists on so many different levels. For this reason alone you defy analysis and tend to remain outside the scope of orthodoxy. And because people can't weigh you up adequately, you appear to be more fascinating than ever.

Aquarius resources

Your chief resource has to be originality. Like a precious Fabergé Egg you are a single creation, unique and quite unlike anything else to be found anywhere in the world. Of course, used wrongly, this can make you seem odd or even downright peculiar. But Aquarians usually have a knack for creating the best possible impression. The chances are that you dress in your own way and speak the words that occur to you, and that you have a side to your nature that shuns convention. Despite this you know how to adapt when necessary. As a result your dinner parties would sport guests of a wide variety of types and stations. All of these people think they know the 'real you' and remain committed to helping you as much as they can.

The natural adaptability that goes along with being an Aquarian makes it possible for you to turn your hand to many different projects. And because you are from an Air sign, you can undertake a variety of tasks at the same time. This makes for a busy life, but being on the go is vital for you and you only tire when you are forced into jobs that you find demeaning, pointless or downright dull.

All of the above combines to make a nature that has 'resourcefulness' as its middle name. Arriving at a given set of circumstances – say a specific task that has to be undertaken – you first analyse what is required. Having done so you get cracking and invariably manage to impress all manner of people with your dexterity, attention to detail and downright intelligence. You can turn work into a social event, or derive financial gain from your social life. Activity is the keyword and you don't really differentiate between the various components of life as many people would.

Success depends on a number of different factors. You need to be doing things you enjoy as much you can and you simply cannot be held back or bound to follow rules that appear to make no sense to you. You respond well to kindness, and generally receive it because you are so considerate yourself. But perhaps your greatest skill of all is your ability to make a silk purse out of a sow's ear. You are never stuck for an idea and rarely let financial restrictions get in your way.

Beneath the surface

'What you see is what you get' could never really be considered a sensible or accurate statement when applied to the sign of Aquarius. It's difficult enough for you to know the way your complicated mind works, and almost impossible for others to sort out the tangle of possibilities. Your mind can be as untidy as a tatty workbox on occasions and yet at other times you can see through situations with a clarity that would dazzle almost any observer. It really depends on a whole host of circumstances, some of which are inevitably beyond your own control. You are at your best when you are allowed to take charge from the very start of any project, because then your originality of thought comes into play. Your sort of logic is unique to you, so don't expect anyone else to go down the same mental routes that you find easy to follow.

Aquarians are naturally kind and don't tend to discriminate. This is not a considered matter, it's simply the way you are. As a result it is very hard for you to understand prejudice, or individuals who show any form of intolerance. The fairness that you exemplify isn't something that you have to work at – it comes as naturally to you as breathing does.

You can be very peculiar and even a little cranky on occasions. These aspects of your nature are unlikely to have any bearing on your overall popularity, but they do betray a rather unusual mindset that isn't like that of any other zodiac sign. When you feel stressed you tend to withdraw into yourself, which is not really good for you. A much better strategy would be to verbalise what you are thinking, even though this is not always particularly easy to do.

There are many people in the world who think they know you well, but each and every one of them knows only one Aquarian. There are always more, each a unique individual and probably as much of a mystery to you as they would be to all your relatives and friends, that is if any of them suspected just how deep and mysterious you can be. Despite these facts, your mind is clear and concise, enabling you to get to the truth of any given situation almost immediately. You should never doubt your intuitive foresight and, in the main, must always back your hunches. It is rare indeed for you to be totally wrong about the outcome of any potential situation and your genuine originality of thought is the greatest gift providence has bestowed on you.

Making the best of yourself

Interacting with the world is most important to you. Although you can sometimes be a good deal quieter than the other Air signs of Gemini and Libra, you are still a born communicator, with a great need to live your life to the full. If you feel hemmed in or constrained by circumstances, you are not going to show your best face to family, friends or colleagues. That's why you must move heaven and earth to make certain that you are not tied down in any way. Maintaining a sense of freedom is really just a mental state to Aquarius but it is absolutely vital to your well-being.

As far as work is concerned you need to be doing something that allows you the room you need to move. Any occupation that means thinking on your feet would probably suit you fine. All the same you feel more comfortable in administrative surroundings, rather than getting your hands dirty. Any profession that brings change and variety on a daily basis would be best. You are a good team operator, and yet can easily lead from the front. Don't be frightened to show colleagues that you have an original way of looking at life and that you are an inveterate problem solver.

In terms of friendship you tend to be quite catholic in your choice of pals. Making the best of yourself means keeping things that way. You are not naturally jealous yourself but you do tend to attract friends who are. Make it plain that you can't tie yourself down to any one association, no matter how old or close it may be. At least if you do this nobody can suggest that they weren't warned when you wander off to talk to someone else. Personal relationships are a different matter, though it's hardly likely that you would live in the pocket of your partner. In any situation you need space to breathe, and this includes romantic attachments. People who know you well will not try to hem you in.

Don't be frightened to show your unconventional, even wild side to the world at large. You are a bold character, with a great deal to say and a natural warmth that could melt an iceberg. This is the way providence made you and it is only right to use your gifts to the full.

The impressions you give

You are not a naturally secretive person and don't hold back very much when it comes to speaking your mind. It might be suggested therefore that the external and internal Aquarian is more or less the same person. Although generally true, it has to be remembered that you have a multi-faceted nature and one that adapts quickly to changing circumstances. It is this very adaptability that sets you apart in the eyes of the world.

You often make decisions based on intuitive foresight and although many Aquarians are of above average intelligence, you won't always make use of a deep knowledge of any given situation. In essence you often do what seems right, though you tend to act whilst others are still standing around and thinking. This makes you good to have around in a crisis and convinces many of those looking on that you are incredibly capable, relaxed and confident. Of course this isn't always the case, but even a nervous interior tends to breed outward action in the case of your zodiac sign, so the world can be forgiven for jumping to the wrong conclusion.

People like you – there's no doubt about that. However, you must realise that you have a very upfront attitude, which on occasions is going to get you into trouble. Your occasional weirdness, rather than being a turn-off, is likely to stimulate the interest that the world has in you. Those with whom you come into contract invariably find your personality to be attractive, generous, high-spirited and refreshing. For all these reasons it is very unlikely that you would actually make many enemies, even if some folk are clearly jealous of the easy way you have with the world.

One of the great things about Aquarians is that they love to join in. As a result you may find yourself doing all sorts of things that others would find either difficult or frightening. You can be zany, wild and even mad on occasions, but these tendencies will only get you liked all the more. The world will only tire of you if you allow yourself to get down in the dumps or grumpy – a very rare state for Aquarius.

The way forward

In terms of living your life to the full it is probable that you don't need any real advice from an astrologer. Your confidence allows you to go places that would make some people shiver, whilst your intuitive foresight gives you the armoury you need to deal with a world that can sometimes seem threatening. Yet for all this you are not immune to mental turmoil on occasions, and probably spend rather too much time in the fast lane. It's good to rest, a fact that you need to remember the next time you find yourself surrounded by twenty-seven jobs, all of which you are trying to undertake at the same time.

The more the world turns in the direction of information technology, the happier you are likely to become. If others have difficulty in this age of computers, it's likely that you relish the challenges and the opportunities that these artificial intelligences offer. You are happy with New Age concepts and tend to look at the world with compassion and understanding. Despite the fact that you are always on the go, it's rare for you to be moving forward so fast that you forget either the planet that brought you to birth, or the many underprivileged people who inhabit parts of it. You have a highly developed conscience and tend to work for the good of humanity whenever you can.

You might not be constructed of the highest moral fibre known to humanity, a fact that sometimes shows when it comes to romantic attachments. Many Aquarians play the field at some time in their lives and it's certain that you need a personal relationship that keeps you mentally stimulated. Although your exterior can sometimes seem superficial, you have a deep and sensitive soul – so perhaps you should marry a poet, or at least someone who can cope with the twists and turns of the Aquarian mind. Aquarians who tie themselves down too early, or to the wrong sort of individual, invariable end up regretting the fact.

You can be deeply creative and need to live in clean and cheerful surroundings. Though not exactly a minimalist you don't like clutter and constantly need to spring-clean your home – and your mind. Living with others isn't difficult for you, in fact it's essential. Since you are so adaptable you fit in easily to almost any environment, though you will always ultimately stamp your own character onto it. You love to be loved and offer a great deal in return, even if you are occasionally absent when people need you the most. In essence you are in love with life and so perhaps you should not be too surprised to discover that it is very fond of you too.

AQUARIUS ON THE CUSP

Astrological profiles are altered for those people born at either the beginning or the end of a zodiac sign, or, more properly, on the cusps of a sign. In the case of Aquarius this would be on the 21st of January and for two or three days after, and similarly at the end of the sign, probably from the 17th to the 19th of February.

The Capricorn Cusp – January 21st to 23rd

What really sets you apart is a genuinely practical streak that isn't always present in the sign of Aquarius when taken alone. You are likely to have all the joy of life and much of the devil-may-care attitude of your Sun sign, but at the same time you are capable of getting things done in a very positive way. This makes you likely to achieve a higher degree of material success and means that you ally managerial skills with the potential for rolling up your sleeves and taking part in the 'real work' yourself. Alongside this you are able to harness the naturally intuitive qualities of Aquarius in a very matter-of-fact way. Few people would have the ability to pull the wool over your eyes and you are rarely stuck for a solution, even to apparently difficult problems.

You express yourself less well than Aquarius taken alone, and you may have a sort of reserve that leads others to believe that your mind is full of still waters which run very deep. The air of mystery can actually be quite useful, because it masks an ability to react and move quickly when necessary, which is a great surprise to the people around you. However, there are two sides to every coin and if there is a slightly negative quality to this cuspid position it might lie in the fact that you are not quite the communicator that tends to be the case with Aquarius, and you could go through some fairly quiet and introspective phases that those around you would find somewhat difficult to understand. In a positive sense this offers a fairly wistful aspect to your nature that may, in romantic applications, appear very attractive. There is something deeply magnetic about your nature and it isn't quite possible for everyone to understand what makes you tick. Actually this is part of your appeal because there is nothing like curiosity on the part of others to enhance your profile.

Getting things done is what matters the most to you, harnessed to the ability to see the wider picture in life. It's true that not everyone understands your complex nature, but in friendship you are scarcely short of supportive types. Family members can be especially important to you and personal attachments are invariably made for life.

The Pisces Cusp – February 17th to 19th

It appears that you are more of a thinker than most and achieve depths of contemplation that would be totally alien to some signs of the zodiac. Much of your life is given over to the service you show for humanity as a whole but you don't sink into the depths of despair in the way that some Piscean individuals are inclined to do. You are immensely likeable and rarely stuck for a good idea. You know how to enjoy yourself, even if this quality is usually tied to the support and assistance that you constantly give to those around you.

Many of you will already have chosen a profession that somehow fulfils your need to be of service, and it isn't unusual for Pisces-cusp Aquarians to alter their path in life totally if it isn't fulfilling this most basic requirement. When necessary, you can turn your hand to almost anything, generally giving yourself totally to the task in hand, sometimes to the exclusion of everything else. People with this combination often have two very different sorts of career, sometimes managing to do both at the same time. Confidence in practical matters isn't usually lacking, even if you sometimes think that your thought processes are a little bit muddled.

In love you are ardent and more sincere than Aquarius sometimes seems to be. There can be a tinge of jealousy at work now and again in deep relationships, but you are less likely than Pisces to let this show. You tend to be very protective of the people who are most important in your life and these are probably fewer in number than often seems to be the case for Aquarius. Your love of humanity and the needs it has of you are of supreme importance and you barely let a day pass without offering some sort of assistance. For this reason, and many others, you are a much loved individual and show your most caring face to the world for the majority of your life. Material success can be hard to come by at first, but it isn't really an aspect of life that worries you too much in any case. It is far more important for you to be content with your lot and, if you are happy, it seems that more or less everything else tends to follow.

AQUARIUS AND ITS ASCENDANTS

The nature of every individual on the planet is composed of the rich variety of zodiac signs and planetary positions that were present at the time of their birth. Your Sun sign, which in your case is Aquarius, is one of the many factors when it comes to assessing the unique person you are. Probably the most important consideration, other than your Sun sign, is to establish the zodiac sign that was rising over the eastern horizon at the time that you were born. This is your Ascending or Rising sign. Most popular astrology fails to take account of the Ascendant, and yet its importance remains with you from the very moment of your birth, through every day of your life. The Ascendant is evident in the way you approach the world, and so, when meeting a person for the first time, it is this astrological influence that you are most likely to notice first. Our Ascending sign essentially represents what we appear to be, while the Sun sign is what we feel inside ourselves.

The Ascendant also has the potential for modifying our overall nature. For example, if you were born at a time of day when Aquarius was passing over the eastern horizon (this would be around the time of dawn) then you would be classed as a double Aquarian. As such, you would typify this zodiac sign, both internally and in your dealings with others. However, if your Ascendant sign turned out to be a Fire sign, such as Aries, there would be a profound alteration of nature, away from the expected qualities of Aquarius.

One of the reasons why popular astrology often ignores the Ascendant is that it has always been rather difficult to establish. We have found a way to make this possible by devising an easy-to-use table, which you will find on page 157 of this book. Using this, you can establish your Ascendant sign at a glance. You will need to know your rough time of birth, then it is simply a case of following the instructions.

For those readers who have no idea of their time of birth it might be worth allowing a good friend, or perhaps your partner, to read through the section that follows this introduction. Someone who deals with you on a regular basis may easily discover your Ascending sign, even though you could have some difficulty establishing it for yourself. A good understanding of this component of your nature is essential if you want to be aware of that 'other person' who is responsible for the way you make contact with the world at large. Your Sun sign, Ascendant sign, and the other pointers in this book will, together, allow you a far better understanding of what makes you tick as an individual. Peeling back the different layers of your astrological make-up can be an enlightening experience, and the Ascendant may represent one of the most important layers of all.

Aquarius with Aquarius Ascendant

You are totally unique and quite original, so much so that very few people could claim to understand what makes you tick. Routines get on your nerves and you need to be out there doing something most of the time. Getting where you want to go in life isn't too difficult, except that when you arrive, your destination might not look half so interesting as it did before. You are well liked and should have many friends. This is not to say that your pals have much in common with each other, because you choose from a wide cross-section of people. Although folks see you as being very reasonable in the main, you are capable of being quite cranky on occasions. Your intuition is extremely strong and is far less likely to let you down than would be the case with some individuals.

Travel is very important to you and you will probably live for some time in a different part of your own country, or even in another part of the world. At work you are more than capable, but do need something to do that you find personally stimulating, because you are not very good at constant routine. You can be relied upon to use your originality and find solutions that are instinctive and brilliant. Most people are very fond of you.

Aquarius with Pisces Ascendant

Here we find the originality of Aquarius balanced by the very sensitive qualities of Pisces, and it makes for a very interesting combination. When it comes to understanding other people you are second to none, but it's certain that you are more instinctive than either Pisces or Aquarius when taken alone. You are better at routines than Aquarius, but also relish a challenge more than the typical Piscean would. Active and enterprising, you tend to know what you want from life, but consideration of others, and the world at large, will always be part of the scenario. People with this combination often work on behalf of humanity and are to be found in social work, the medical profession and religious institutions. As far as beliefs are concerned you don't conform to established patterns, and yet may get closer to the truth of the Creator than many deep theological thinkers have ever been able to do. Acting on impulse as much as you do means that not everyone understands the way your mind works, but your popularity will invariably see you through.

Passionate and deeply sensitive, you are able to negotiate the twists and turns of a romantic life that is hardly likely to be run-of-the-mill. In the end, however, you should be able to discover a very deep personal and spiritual happiness.

Aquarius with Aries Ascendant

If ever anyone could be accused of setting off immediately, but slowly, it has to be you. These are very contradictory signs and the differences will express themselves in a variety of ways. One thing is certain, you have tremendous tenacity and will see a job through patiently from beginning to end, without tiring on the way and ensuring that every detail is taken care of properly. This combination often brings good health and a great capacity for continuity, particularly in terms of the length of life. You are certainly not as argumentative as the typical Aries, but you do know how to get your own way, which is just as well because you are usually thinking on behalf of everyone else and not just on your own account.

At home you can relax, which is a blessing for Aries, though in fact you seldom choose to do so because you always have some project or other on the go. You probably enjoy knocking down and rebuilding walls, though this is a practical tendency and not responsive to relationships, in which you are ardent and sincere. Impetuosity is as close to your heart as is the case for any type of subject, though you certainly have the ability to appear patient and steady. But it's just a front, isn't it?

Aquarius with Taurus Ascendant

There is nothing that you fail to think about deeply and with great intensity. You are wise, honest and very scientific in your approach to life. Routines are necessary in life but you have most of them sorted out well in advance and so always have time to look at the next interesting fact. If you don't spend all your time watching documentaries on the television set, you make a good friend and love to socialise. Most of the great discoveries of the world were probably made by people with this sort of astrological combination, though your nature is rather 'odd' on occasions and so can be rather difficult for others to understand.

You may be most surprised when others tell you that you are eccentric, but you don't really mind too much because for half of the time you are not inhabiting the same world as the rest of us. Because you can be delightfully dotty you are probably much loved and cherished by your friends, of which there are likely to be many. Family members probably adore you too, and you can be guaranteed to entertain anyone with whom you come into contact. The only fly in the ointment is that you sometimes lose track of reality, whatever that might be, and fly high in your own atmosphere of rarefied possibilities.

Aquarius with Gemini Ascendant

If you were around in the 1960s there is every chance that you were the first to go around with flowers in your hair. You are unconventional, original, quirky and entertaining. Few people would fail to notice your presence and you take life as it comes, even though on most occasions you are firmly in the driving seat. It all probability you care very much about the planet on which you live and the people with whom you share it. Not everyone understands you, but that does not really matter, for you have more than enough communication skills to put your message across intact. You should avoid wearing yourself out by worrying about things that you cannot control, and you definitely gain from taking time out to meditate. However, whether or not you allow yourself that luxury remains to be seen.

If you are not the most communicative form of Gemini subject then you must come a close second. Despite this fact much of what you have to say makes real sense and you revel in the company of interesting, intelligent and stimulating people, whose opinions on a host of matters will add to your own considerations. You are a true original in every sense of the word and the mere fact of your presence in the world is bound to add to the enjoyment of life experienced by the many people with whom you make contact.

Aquarius with Cancer Ascendant

The truly original spark, for which the sign of Aquarius is famed, can only enhance the caring qualities of Cancer, and is also inclined to bring the Crab out of its shell to a much greater extent than would be the case with certain other zodiac combinations. Aquarius is a party animal and never arrives without something interesting to say, which is doubly the case when the reservoir of emotion and consideration that is Cancer is feeding the tap. Your nature can be rather confusing for even you to deal with, but you are inspirational, bright, charming and definitely fun to be around.

The Cancer element in your nature means that you care about your home and the people to whom you are related. You are also a good and loyal friend, who would keep attachments for much longer than could be expected for Aquarius alone. You love to travel and can be expected to make many journeys to far-off places during your life. Some attention will have to be paid to your health, because you are capable of burning up masses of nervous energy, often without getting the periods of rest and contemplation that are essential to the deeper qualities of the sign of Cancer. Nevertheless you have determination, resilience and a refreshing attitude that lifts the spirits of the people in your vicinity.

Aquarius with Leo Ascendant

All associations with Aquarius bring originality, and you are no exception. You aspire to do your best most of the time but manage to achieve your objectives in an infinitely amusing and entertaining way. Not that you set out to do so, because if you are an actor on the stage of life, it seems as though you are a natural one. There is nothing remotely pretentious about your breezy personality or your ability to occupy the centre of any stage. This analogy is quite appropriate because you probably like the theatre. Being in any situation when reality is suspended for a while suits you down to the ground, and in any case you may regularly ask yourself if you even recognise what reality is. Always asking questions, both of yourself and the world at large, you soldier on relentlessly, though not to the exclusion of having a good time on the way.

Keeping to tried and tested paths is not your way. You are a natural trailblazer who is full of good ideas and who has the energy to put them into practice. You care deeply for the people who play an important part in your life but are wise enough to allow them the space they need to develop their own personalities along the way. Most people like you, many love you, and one or two think that you really are the best thing since sliced bread.

Aquarius with Virgo Ascendant

How could anyone make the convention unconventional? Well, if anyone can manage, you can. There are great contradictions here, because on the one hand you always want to do the expected thing, but the Aquarian quality within your nature loves to surprise everyone on the way. If you don't always know what you are thinking or doing, it's a pretty safe bet that others won't either, so it's important on occasions really to stop and think. However this is not a pressing concern, because you tend to live a fairly happy life and muddle through no matter what. Other people tend to take to you well and it is likely that you will have many friends. You tend to be bright and cheerful and can approach even difficult tasks with the certainty that you have the skills necessary to see them through to their conclusion. Give and take are important factors in the life of any individual and particularly so in your case. Because you can stretch yourself in order to understand what makes other people think and act in the way that they do, you have the reputation of being a good friend and a reliable colleague.

In love you can be somewhat more fickle than the typical Virgoan, and yet you are always interesting to live with. Where you are, things happen, and you mix a sparkling wit with deep insights.

Aquarius with Libra Ascendant

Stand by for a truly interesting and very inspiring combination here, but one that is sometimes rather difficult to fathom, even for the sort of people who believe themselves to be very perceptive. The reason for this could be that any situation has to be essentially fixed and constant in order to get a handle on it, and this is certainly not the case for the Aquarian–Libran type. The fact is that both these signs are Air signs, and to a certain extent as unpredictable as the wind itself.

To most people you seem to be original, frank, free and very outspoken. Not everything you do makes sense to others and if you were alive during the hippy era, it is likely that you went around with flowers in your hair, for you are a free-thinking idealist at heart. With age you mature somewhat, but never too much, because you will always see the strange, the comical and the original in life. This is what keeps you young and is one of the factors that makes you so very attractive to members of the opposite sex. Many people will want to 'adopt' you and you are at your very best when in company. Much of your effort is expounded on others and yet, unless you discipline yourself a good deal, personal relationships of the romantic sort can bring certain difficulties. Careful planning is necessary.

Aquarius with Scorpio Ascendant

Here we have a combination that shows much promise and a
flexibility that allows many changes in direction, allied to a power to
succeed, sometimes very much against all the odds. Aquarius
lightens the load of the Scorpio mind, turning the depths into
potential, and intuitive foresight into a means for getting on in life.
There are depths here, because even airy Aquarius isn't so easy to
understand, and it is therefore a fact that some people with this
combination will always be something of a mystery. However, even
this fact can be turned to your advantage because it means that
people will always be looking at you. Confidence is so often the key
to success in life and the Scorpio–Aquarius mix offers this, or at least
appears to do so. Even when this is not entirely the case, the fact
that everyone around you believes it to be true is often enough.

You are usually good to know, and show a keen intellect and a
deep intelligence, aided by a fascination for life that knows no
bounds. When at your best you are giving, understanding, balanced
and active. On those occasions when things are not going well for
you, beware of a stubborn streak and the need to be sensational.
Keep it light and happy and you won't go far wrong. Most of you
are very, very much loved.

Aquarius with Sagittarius Ascendant

There is an original streak to your nature which is very attractive to the people with whom you share your life. Always different, ever on the go and anxious to try out the next experiment in life, you are interested in almost everything, and yet deeply attached to almost nothing. Everyone you know thinks that you are a little 'odd', but you probably don't mind them believing this because you know it to be true. In fact it is possible that you positively relish your eccentricity, which sets you apart from the common herd and means that you are always going to be noticed.

Although it may seem strange with this combination of Air and Fire, you can be distinctly cool on occasions, have a deep and abiding love of your own company now and again and won't be easily understood. Love comes fairly easily to you but there are times when you are accused of being self-possessed, self-indulgent and not willing enough to fall in line with the wishes of those around you. Despite this you walk on and on down your own path. At heart you are an extrovert and you love to party, often late into the night. Luxury appeals to you, though it tends to be of the transient sort. Travel could easily play a major and a very important part in your life.

Aquarius with Capricorn Ascendant

Here the determination of Capricorn is assisted by a slightly more adaptable quality and an off-beat personality that tends to keep everyone else guessing. You don't care to be quite so predictable as the archetypal Capricorn would be, and there is a more idealistic quality here, or at least one that shows more. A greater number of friends than Capricorn usually keeps is likely, though less than the true Aquarian would gather. Few people doubt your sincerity, though by no means all of them understand what makes you tick. Unfortunately you are not in a position to help them out, because you are not too sure yourself. All the same, you muddle through and can be very capable when the mood takes you.

Being a natural traveller, you love to see new places and would be quite fascinated by cultures that are very different to your own. People with this combination are inclined to spend some time living abroad and may even settle there. You look out for the underdog and will always have time for a good cause, no matter what it takes to help. In romantic terms you are a reliable partner, though with a slightly wayward edge which, if anything, tends to make you even more attractive. Listen to your intuition, which is well honed and rarely lets you down. Generally speaking you are very popular.

THE MOON AND THE PART IT PLAYS IN YOUR LIFE

In astrology the Moon is probably the single most important heavenly body after the Sun. Its unique position, as partner to the Earth on its journey around the solar system, means that the Moon appears to pass through the signs of the zodiac extremely quickly. The zodiac position of the Moon at the time of your birth plays a great part in personal character and is especially significant in the build-up of your emotional nature.

Your Own Moon Sign

Discovering the position of the Moon at the time of your birth has always been notoriously difficult because tracking the complex zodiac positions of the Moon is not easy. This process has been reduced to three simple stages with our Lunar Tables. A breakdown of the Moon's zodiac positions can be found from page 35 onwards, so that once you know what your Moon Sign is, you can see what part this plays in the overall build-up of your personal character.

If you follow the instructions on the next page you will soon be able to work out exactly what zodiac sign the Moon occupied on the day that you were born and you can then go on to compare the reading for this position with those of your Sun sign and your Ascendant. It is partly the comparison between these three important positions that goes towards making you the unique individual you are.

HOW TO DISCOVER YOUR MOON SIGN

This is a three-stage process. You may need a pen and a piece of paper but if you follow the instructions below the process should only take a minute or so.

STAGE 1 First of all you need to know the Moon Age at the time of your birth. If you look at Moon Table 1, on page 33, you will find all the years between 1911 and 2009 down the left side. Find the year of your birth and then trace across to the right to the month of your birth. Where the two intersect you will find a number. This is the date of the New Moon in the month that you were born. You now need to count forward the number of days between the New Moon and your own birthday. For example, if the New Moon in the month of your birth was shown as being the 6th and you were born on the 20th, your Moon Age Day would be 14. If the New Moon in the month of your birth came after your birthday, you need to count forward from the New Moon in the previous month. If you were born in a Leap Year, remember to count the 29th February. You can tell if your birth year was a Leap Year if the last two digits can be divided by four. Whatever the result, jot this number down so that you do not forget it.

STAGE 2 Take a look at Moon Table 2 on page 34. Down the left hand column look for the date of your birth. Now trace across to the month of your birth. Where the two meet you will find a letter. Copy this letter down alongside your Moon Age Day.

STAGE 3 Moon Table 3 on page 34 will supply you with the zodiac sign the Moon occupied on the day of your birth. Look for your Moon Age Day down the left hand column and then for the letter you found in Stage 2. Where the two converge you will find a zodiac sign and this is the sign occupied by the Moon on the day that you were born.

Your Zodiac Moon Sign Explained

You will find a profile of all zodiac Moon Signs on pages 35 to 38, showing in yet another way how astrology helps to make you into the individual that you are. In each daily entry of the Astral Diary you can find the zodiac position of the Moon for every day of the year. This also allows you to discover your lunar birthdays. Since the Moon passes through all the signs of the zodiac in about a month, you can expect something like twelve lunar birthdays each year. At these times you are likely to be emotionally steady and able to make the sort of decisions that have real, lasting value.

MOON TABLE 1

YEAR	DEC	JAN	FEB	YEAR	DEC	JAN	FEB	YEAR	DEC	JAN	FEB
1911	20	29	28	1944	15	25	24	1977	10	19	18
1912	9	18	17	1945	4	14	12	1978	29	9	7
1913	27	7	6	1946	23	3	2	1979	18	27	26
1914	17	25	24	1947	12	21	19	1980	7	16	15
1915	6	15	14	1948	1/30	11	9	1981	26	6	4
1916	25	5	3	1949	19	29	27	1982	15	25	23
1917	13	24	22	1950	9	18	16	1983	4	14	13
1918	2	12	11	1951	28	7	6	1984	22	3	1
1919	21	1/31	–	1952	17	26	25	1985	12	21	19
1920	10	20	19	1953	6	15	14	1986	1/30	10	9
1921	29	9	8	1954	25	5	3	1987	20	29	28
1922	18	27	26	1955	14	24	22	1988	9	19	17
1923	8	17	15	1956	2	13	11	1989	28	7	6
1924	26	6	5	1957	21	1/30	–	1990	17	26	25
1925	15	24	23	1958	10	19	18	1991	6	15	14
1926	5	14	12	1959	29	9	7	1992	24	4	3
1927	24	3	2	1960	18	27	26	1993	14	23	22
1928	12	21	19	1961	7	16	15	1994	2	11	10
1929	1/30	11	9	1962	26	6	5	1995	22	1/30	–
1930	19	29	28	1963	15	25	23	1996	10	20	18
1931	9	18	17	1964	4	14	13	1997	28	9	7
1932	27	7	6	1965	22	3	1	1998	18	27	26
1933	17	25	24	1966	12	21	19	1999	7	17	16
1934	6	15	14	1967	1/30	10	9	2000	26	6	4
1935	25	5	3	1968	20	29	28	2001	15	25	23
1936	13	24	22	1969	9	19	17	2002	4	13	12
1937	2	12	11	1970	28	7	6	2003	23	3	1
1938	21	1/31	–	1971	17	26	25	2004	11	21	20
1939	10	20	19	1972	6	15	14	2005	30	10	9
1940	28	9	8	1973	25	5	4	2006	20	29	28
1941	18	27	26	1974	14	24	22	2007	9	18	16
1942	8	16	15	1975	3	12	11	2008	27	8	6
1943	27	6	4	1976	21	1/31	29	2009	16	26	25

TABLE 2

MOON TABLE 3

DAY	JAN	FEB	M/D	A	B	C	D	E	F	G
1	A	D	0	CP	AQ	AQ	AQ	PI	PI	PI
2	A	D	1	AQ	AQ	AQ	PI	PI	PI	AR
3	A	D	2	AQ	AQ	PI	PI	PI	AR	AR
4	A	D	3	AQ	PI	PI	PI	AR	AR	AR
5	A	D	4	PI	PI	AR	AR	AR	AR	TA
6	A	D	5	PI	AR	AR	AR	TA	TA	TA
7	A	D	6	AR	AR	AR	TA	TA	TA	GE
8	A	D	7	AR	AR	TA	TA	TA	GE	GE
9	A	D	8	AR	TA	TA	TA	GE	GE	GE
10	A	E	9	TA	TA	GE	GE	GE	CA	CA
11	B	E	10	TA	GE	GE	GE	CA	CA	CA
12	B	E	11	GE	GE	GE	CA	CA	CA	LE
13	B	E	12	GE	GE	CA	CA	CA	LE	LE
14	B	E	13	GE	CA	CA	LE	LE	LE	LE
15	B	E	14	CA	CA	LE	LE	LE	VI	VI
16	B	E	15	CA	LE	LE	LE	VI	VI	VI
17	B	E	16	LE	LE	LE	VI	VI	VI	LI
18	B	E	17	LE	LE	VI	VI	VI	LI	LI
19	B	E	18	LE	VI	VI	VI	LI	LI	LI
20	B	F	19	VI	VI	VI	LI	LI	LI	SC
21	C	F	20	VI	LI	LI	LI	SC	SC	SC
22	C	F	21	LI	LI	LI	SC	SC	SC	SA
23	C	F	22	LI	LI	SC	SC	SC	SA	SA
24	C	F	23	LI	SC	SC	SC	SA	SA	SA
25	C	F	24	SC	SC	SC	SA	SA	SA	CP
26	C	F	25	SC	SA	SA	SA	CP	CP	CP
27	C	F	26	SA	SA	SA	CP	CP	CP	AQ
28	C	F	27	SA	SA	CP	CP	AQ	AQ	AQ
29	C	F	28	SA	CP	CP	AQ	AQ	AQ	AQ
30	C	–	29	CP	CP	CP	AQ	AQ	AQ	PI
31	D	–								

AR = Aries, TA = Taurus, GE = Gemini, CA = Cancer, LE = Leo, VI = Virgo, LI = Libra, SC = Scorpio, SA = Sagittarius, CP = Capricorn, AQ = Aquarius, PI = Pisces

MOON SIGNS

Moon in Aries

You have a strong imagination, courage, determination and a desire to do things in your own way and forge your own path through life.

Originality is a key attribute; you are seldom stuck for ideas although your mind is changeable and you could take the time to focus on individual tasks. Often quick-tempered, you take orders from few people and live life at a fast pace. Avoid health problems by taking regular time out for rest and relaxation.

Emotionally, it is important that you talk to those you are closest to and work out your true feelings. Once you discover that people are there to help, there is less necessity for you to do everything yourself.

Moon in Taurus

The Moon in Taurus gives you a courteous and friendly manner, which means you are likely to have many friends.

The good things in life mean a lot to you, as Taurus is an Earth sign that delights in experiences which please the senses. Hence you are probably a lover of good food and drink, which may in turn mean you need to keep an eye on the bathroom scales, especially as looking good is also important to you.

Emotionally you are fairly stable and you stick by your own standards. Taureans do not respond well to change. Intuition also plays an important part in your life.

Moon in Gemini

You have a warm-hearted character, sympathetic and eager to help others. At times reserved, you can also be articulate and chatty: this is part of the paradox of Gemini, which always brings duplicity to the nature. You are interested in current affairs, have a good intellect, and are good company and likely to have many friends. Most of your friends have a high opinion of you and would be ready to defend you should the need arise. However, this is usually unnecessary, as you are quite capable of defending yourself in any verbal confrontation.

Travel is important to your inquisitive mind and you find intellectual stimulus in mixing with people from different cultures. You also gain much from reading, writing and the arts but you do need plenty of rest and relaxation in order to avoid fatigue.

Moon in Cancer

The Moon in Cancer at the time of birth is a fortunate position as Cancer is the Moon's natural home. This means that the qualities of compassion and understanding given by the Moon are especially enhanced in your nature, and you are friendly and sociable and cope well with emotional pressures. You cherish home and family life, and happily do the domestic tasks. Your surroundings are important to you and you hate squalor and filth. You are likely to have a love of music and poetry.

Your basic character, although at times changeable like the Moon itself, depends on symmetry. You aim to make your surroundings comfortable and harmonious, for yourself and those close to you.

Moon in Leo

The best qualities of the Moon and Leo come together to make you warm-hearted, fair, ambitious and self-confident. With good organisational abilities, you invariably rise to a position of responsibility in your chosen career. This is fortunate as you don't enjoy being an 'also-ran' and would rather be an important part of a small organisation than a menial in a large one.

You should be lucky in love, and happy, provided you put in the effort to make a comfortable home for yourself and those close to you. It is likely that you will have a love of pleasure, sport, music and literature. Life brings you many rewards, most of them as a direct result of your own efforts, although you may be luckier than average and ready to make the best of any situation.

Moon in Virgo

You are endowed with good mental abilities and a keen receptive memory, but you are never ostentatious or pretentious. Naturally quite reserved, you still have many friends, especially of the opposite sex. Marital relationships must be discussed carefully and worked at so that they remain harmonious, as personal attachments can be a problem if you do not give them your full attention.

Talented and persevering, you possess artistic qualities and are a good homemaker. Earning your honours through genuine merit, you work long and hard towards your objectives but show little pride in your achievements. Many short journeys will be undertaken in your life.

Moon in Libra

With the Moon in Libra you are naturally popular and make friends easily. People like you, probably more than you realise, you bring fun to a party and are a natural diplomat. For all its good points, Libra is not the most stable of astrological signs and, as a result, your emotions can be a little unstable too. Therefore, although the Moon in Libra is said to be good for love and marriage, your Sun sign and Rising sign will have an important effect on your emotional and loving qualities.

You must remember to relate to others in your decision-making. Co-operation is crucial because Libra represents the 'balance' of life that can only be achieved through harmonious relationships. Conformity is not easy for you because Libra, an Air sign, likes its independence.

Moon in Scorpio

Some people might call you pushy. In fact, all you really want to do is to live life to the full and protect yourself and your family from the pressures of life. Take care to avoid giving the impression of being sarcastic or impulsive and use your energies wisely and constructively.

You have great courage and you invariably achieve your goals by force of personality and sheer effort. You are fond of mystery and are good at predicting the outcome of situations and events. Travel experiences can be beneficial to you.

You may experience problems if you do not take time to examine your motives in a relationship, and also if you allow jealousy, always a feature of Scorpio, to cloud your judgement.

Moon in Sagittarius

The Moon in Sagittarius helps to make you a generous individual with humanitarian qualities and a kind heart. Restlessness may be intrinsic as your mind is seldom still. Perhaps because of this, you have a need for change that could lead you to several major moves during your adult life. You are not afraid to stand your ground when you know your judgement is right, you speak directly and have good intuition.

At work you are quick, efficient and versatile and so you make an ideal employee. You need work to be intellectually demanding and do not enjoy tedious routines.

In relationships, you anger quickly if faced with stupidity or deception, though you are just as quick to forgive and forget. Emotionally, there are times when your heart rules your head.

37

Moon in Capricorn

The Moon in Capricorn makes you popular and likely to come into the public eye in some way. The watery Moon is not entirely comfortable in the Earth sign of Capricorn and this may lead to some difficulties in the early years of life. An initial lack of creative ability and indecision must be overcome before the true qualities of patience and perseverance inherent in Capricorn can show through.

You have good administrative ability and are a capable worker, and if you are careful you can accumulate wealth. But you must be cautious and take professional advice in partnerships, as you are open to deception. You may be interested in social or welfare work, which suit your organisational skills and sympathy for others.

Moon in Aquarius

The Moon in Aquarius makes you an active and agreeable person with a friendly, easy-going nature. Sympathetic to the needs of others, you flourish in a laid-back atmosphere. You are broad-minded, fair and open to suggestion, although sometimes you have an unconventional quality which others can find hard to understand.

You are interested in the strange and curious, and in old articles and places. You enjoy trips to these places and gain much from them. Political, scientific and educational work interests you and you might choose a career in science or technology.

Money-wise, you make gains through innovation and concentration and Lunar Aquarians often tackle more than one job at a time. In love you are kind and honest.

Moon in Pisces

You have a kind, sympathetic nature, somewhat retiring at times, but you always take account of others' feelings and help when you can.

Personal relationships may be problematic, but as life goes on you can learn from your experiences and develop a better understanding of yourself and the world around you.

You have a fondness for travel, appreciate beauty and harmony and hate disorder and strife. You may be fond of literature and would make a good writer or speaker yourself. You have a creative imagination and may come across as an incurable romantic. You have strong intuition, maybe bordering on a mediumistic quality, which sets you apart from the mass. You may not be rich in cash terms, but your personal gifts are worth more than gold.

AQUARIUS IN LOVE

Discover how compatible in love you are with people from the same and other signs of the zodiac. Five stars equals a match made in heaven!

Aquarius meets Aquarius

This is a good match for several reasons. Most importantly, although it sounds arrogant, Aquarians like themselves. At its best, Aquarius is one of the fairest, most caring and genuinely pleasant zodiac signs and so it is only when faced by the difficulties created by others that it shows a less favourable side. Put two Aquarians together and voilà – instant success! Personal and family life should bring more joy. On the whole, a platform for adventure based on solid foundations. Star rating: *****

Aquarius meets Pisces

Zodiac signs that follow each other often have something in common, but this is not the case with Aquarius and Pisces. Both signs are deeply caring, but in different ways. Pisces is one of the deepest zodiac signs, and Aquarius simply isn't prepared to embark on the journey. Pisceans, meanwhile, would probably find Aquarians superficial and even flippant. On the positive side there is potential for a well-balanced relationship, but unless one party is untypical of their zodiac sign, it often doesn't get started. Star rating: **

Aquarius meets Aries

Aquarius is an Air sign, and Air and Fire often work well together, but not in the case of Aries and Aquarius. The average Aquarian lives in what the Ram sees as a fantasy world, so a meeting of minds is unlikely. Of course, the dominant side of Aries could be trained by the devil-may-care attitude of Aquarius. There are meeting points but they are difficult to establish. However, given sufficient time and an open mind on both sides, a degree of happiness is possible. Star rating: **

Aquarius meets Taurus

In any relationship of which Aquarius is a part, surprises abound. It is difficult for Taurus to understand the soul-searching, adventurous, changeable Aquarian, but on the positive side, the Bull is adaptable and can respond well to a dose of excitement. Aquarians are kind and react well to the same quality coming back at them. Both are friendly, capable of deep affection and basically creative. Unfortunately, Taurus simply doesn't know what makes Aquarius tick, which could lead to feelings of isolation, even if these don't always show on the surface. Star rating: **

Aquarius meets Gemini

Aquarius is commonly mistaken for a Water sign, but in fact it's ruled by the Air element, and this is the key to its compatibility with Gemini. Both signs mix freely socially, and each has an insatiable curiosity. There is plenty of action, lots of love, but very little rest, and so great potential for success if they don't wear each other out! Aquarius revels in its own eccentricity, and encourages Gemini to emulate this. Theirs will be an unconventional household, but almost everyone warms to this crazy and unpredictable couple. Star rating: *****

Aquarius meets Cancer

Cancer is often attracted to Aquarius and, as Aquarius is automatically on the side of anyone who fancies it, so there is the potential for something good here. Cancer loves Aquarius' devil-may-care approach to life, but also recognises and seeks to strengthen the basic lack of self-confidence that all Air signs try so hard to keep secret. Both signs are natural travellers and are quite adventurous. Their family life could be unusual, but friends would recognise a caring, sharing household with many different interests shared by people genuinely in love. Star rating: ***

Aquarius meets Leo

The problem here is that Aquarius doesn't think in the general sense of the word, it knows. Leo, on the other hand, is more practical and relies more on logical reasoning, and consequently it doesn't understand Aquarius very well. Aquarians can also appear slightly frosty in their appreciation of others and this, too, will annoy Leo. This is a good match for a business partnership because Aquarius is astute, while Leo is brave, but personally the prognosis is less promising. Tolerance, understanding and forbearance are all needed to make this work. Star rating: **

Aquarius meets Virgo

Aquarius is a strange sign because no matter how well one knows it, it always manages to surprise. For this reason, against the odds, it's quite likely that Aquarius will form a sucessful relationship with Virgo. Aquarius is changeable, unpredictable and often quite odd, while Virgo is steady, a fuss-pot and very practical. Herein lies the key. What one sign needs, the other provides and that may be the surest recipe for success imaginable. On-lookers may not know why the couple are happy, but they will recognise that this is the case. Star rating: ****

Aquarius meets Libra

One of the best combinations imaginable, partly because both are Air signs and so share a common meeting point. But perhaps the more crucial factor is that both signs respect each other. Aquarius loves life and originality, and is quite intellectual. Libra is similar, but more balanced and rather less eccentric. A visit to this couple's house would be entertaining and full of zany wit, activity and excitement. Both are keen to travel and may prefer to 'find themselves' before taking on too many domestic responsibilities. Star rating: *****

Aquarius meets Scorpio

This is a promising and practical combination. Scorpio responds well to Aquarius' persistent exploration of its deep nature and so this generally shy sign becomes lighter, brighter and more inspirational. Meanwhile, Aquarians are rarely as sure of themselves as they like to appear and are reassured by Scorpio's constant, steady and determined support. Both signs want to be kind to each other, which is a good starting point to a relationship that should be warm most of the time and extremely hot occasionally. Star rating: ****

Aquarius meets Sagittarius

Both Sagittarius and Aquarius are into mind games, which may lead to something of an intellectual competition. If one side is happy to be 'bamboozled' it won't be a problem, but it is more likely that the relationship will turn into a competition, which won't auger well for its long-term future. However, on the plus side, both signs are adventurous and sociable, so as long as there is always something new and interesting to do, the match could turn out very well. Star rating: **

Aquarius meets Capricorn

Probably one of the least likely combinations, as Capricorn and Aquarius are unlikely to choose each other in the first place, unless one side is quite untypical of their sign. Capricorn approaches things in a practical way and likes to get things done, while Aquarius works almost exclusively for the moment and relies heavily on intuition. Their attitudes to romance are also diametrically opposed: Aquarius' moods tend to swing from red hot to ice cold in a minute, which is alien to steady Capricorn. Star rating: **

VENUS:
THE PLANET OF LOVE

If you look up at the sky around sunset or sunrise you will often see Venus in close attendance to the Sun. It is arguably one of the most beautiful sights of all and there is little wonder that historically it became associated with the goddess of love. But although Venus does play an important part in the way you view love and in the way others see you romantically, this is only one of the spheres of influence that it enjoys in your overall character.

Venus has a part to play in the more cultured side of your life and has much to do with your appreciation of art, literature, music and general creativity. Even the way you look is responsive to the part of the zodiac that Venus occupied at the start of your life, though this fact is also down to your Sun sign and Ascending sign. If, at the time you were born, Venus occupied one of the more gregarious zodiac signs, you will be more likely to wear your heart on your sleeve, as well as to be more attracted to entertainment, social gatherings and good company. If on the other hand Venus occupied a quiet zodiac sign at the time of your birth, you would tend to be more retiring and less willing to shine in public situations.

It's good to know what part the planet Venus plays in your life for it can have a great bearing on the way you appear to the rest of the world and since we all have to mix with others, you can learn to make the very best of what Venus has to offer you.

One of the great complications in the past has always been trying to establish exactly what zodiac position Venus enjoyed when you were born because the planet is notoriously difficult to track. However, we have solved that problem by creating a table that is exclusive to your Sun sign, which you will find on the following page.

Establishing your Venus sign could not be easier. Just look up the year of your birth on the following page and you will see a sign of the zodiac. This was the sign that Venus occupied in the period covered by your sign in that year. If Venus occupied more than one sign during the period, this is indicated by the date on which the sign changed, and the name of the new sign. For instance, if you were born in 1945, Venus was in Pisces until the 12th February, after which time it was in Aries. If you were born before 12th February your Venus sign is Pisces, if you were born on or after 12th February, your Venus sign is Aries. Once you have established the position of Venus at the time of your birth, you can then look in the pages which follow to see how this has a bearing on your life as a whole.

1911 AQUARIUS / 3.2 PISCES
1912 SAGITTARIUS / 30.1 CAPRICORN
1913 PISCES / 16.2 ARIES
1914 CAPRICORN / 26.1 AQUARIUS /
   19.2 PISCES
1915 SAGITTARIUS / 7.2 CAPRICORN
1916 PISCES / 14.2 ARIES
1917 CAPRICORN / 9.2 AQUARIUS
1918 AQUARIUS
1919 AQUARIUS / 3.2 PISCES
1920 SAGITTARIUS / 30.1 CAPRICORN
1921 PISCES / 15.2 ARIES
1922 CAPRICORN / 25.1 AQUARIUS /
   18.2 PISCES
1923 SAGITTARIUS / 7.2 CAPRICORN
1924 PISCES / 13.2 ARIES
1925 CAPRICORN / 9.2 AQUARIUS
1926 AQUARIUS
1927 AQUARIUS / 2.2 PISCES
1928 SAGITTARIUS / 29.1 CAPRICORN
1929 PISCES / 14.2 ARIES
1930 CAPRICORN / 25.1 AQUARIUS /
   18.2 PISCES
1931 SAGITTARIUS / 6.2 CAPRICORN
1932 PISCES / 13.2 ARIES
1933 CAPRICORN / 8.2 AQUARIUS
1934 AQUARIUS
1935 AQUARIUS / 2.2 PISCES
1936 SAGITTARIUS / 29.1 CAPRICORN
1937 PISCES / 13.2 ARIES
1938 CAPRICORN / 24.1 AQUARIUS /
   17.2 PISCES
1939 SAGITTARIUS / 6.2 CAPRICORN
1940 PISCES / 12.2 ARIES
1941 CAPRICORN / 8.2 AQUARIUS
1942 AQUARIUS
1943 AQUARIUS / 1.2 PISCES
1944 SAGITTARIUS / 28.1 CAPRICORN
1945 PISCES / 12.2 ARIES
1946 CAPRICORN / 24.1 AQUARIUS /
   17.2 PISCES
1947 SAGITTARIUS / 6.2 CAPRICORN
1948 PISCES / 12.2 ARIES
1949 CAPRICORN / 7.2 AQUARIUS
1950 AQUARIUS
1951 AQUARIUS / 1.2 PISCES
1952 SAGITTARIUS / 27.1 CAPRICORN
1953 PISCES / 11.2 ARIES
1954 CAPRICORN / 23.1 AQUARIUS /
   16.2 PISCES
1955 SAGITTARIUS / 6.2 CAPRICORN
1956 PISCES / 11.2 ARIES
1957 CAPRICORN / 7.2 AQUARIUS
1958 AQUARIUS
1959 AQUARIUS / 31.1 PISCES
1960 SAGITTARIUS / 27.1 CAPRICORN
1961 PISCES / 9.2 ARIES

1962 CAPRICORN / 23.1 AQUARIUS /
   15.2 PISCES
1963 SAGITTARIUS / 6.2 CAPRICORN
1964 PISCES / 11.2 ARIES
1965 CAPRICORN / 6.2 AQUARIUS
1966 AQUARIUS
1967 AQUARIUS / 30.1 PISCES
1968 SAGITTARIUS / 26.1 CAPRICORN
1969 PISCES / 7.2 ARIES
1970 CAPRICORN / 22.1 AQUARIUS /
   15.2 PISCES
1971 SAGITTARIUS / 5.2 CAPRICORN
1972 PISCES / 10.2 ARIES
1973 CAPRICORN / 5.2 AQUARIUS
1974 AQUARIUS / 7.2 CAPRICORN
1975 AQUARIUS / 30.1 PISCES
1976 SAGITTARIUS / 26.1 CAPRICORN
1977 PISCES / 5.2 ARIES
1978 CAPRICORN / 22.1 AQUARIUS /
   14.2 PISCES
1979 SAGITTARIUS / 5.2 CAPRICORN
1980 PISCES / 10.2 ARIES
1981 CAPRICORN / 5.2 AQUARIUS
1982 AQUARIUS / 29.1 CAPRICORN
1983 AQUARIUS / 29.1 CAPRICORN
1984 SAGITTARIUS / 25.1 CAPRICORN
1985 PISCES / 5.2 ARIES
1986 AQUARIUS / 14.2 PISCES
1987 SAGITTARIUS / 5.2 CAPRICORN
1988 PISCES / 9.2 ARIES
1989 CAPRICORN / 4.2 AQUARIUS
1990 AQUARIUS / 23.1 CAPRICORN
1991 AQUARIUS / 29.1 PISCES
1992 SAGITTARIUS / 25.1 CAPRICORN
1993 PISCES / 4.2 ARIES
1994 AQUARIUS / 13.2 PISCES
1995 SAGITTARIUS / 5.2 CAPRICORN
1996 PISCES / 9.2 ARIES
1997 CAPRICORN / 4.2 AQUARIUS
1998 AQUARIUS / 23.1 CAPRICORN
1999 AQUARIUS / 29.1 PISCES
2000 SAGITTARIUS / 25.1 CAPRICORN
2001 PISCES / 4.2 ARIES
2002 AQUARIUS / 13.2 PISCES
2003 SAGITTARIUS
2004 PISCES / 9.2 AQUARIUS
2005 CAPRICORN / 6.2 AQUARIUS
2006 AQUARIUS / 14.01 CAPRICORN
2007 AQUARIUS / 19.01 PISCES
2008 SAGITTARIUS / 25.1 CAPRICORN
2009 PISCES / 4.2 ARIES

VENUS THROUGH THE ZODIAC SIGNS

Venus in Aries

Amongst other things, the position of Venus in Aries indicates a fondness for travel, music and all creative pursuits. Your nature tends to be affectionate and you would try not to create confusion or difficulty for others if it could be avoided. Many people with this planetary position have a great love of the theatre, and mental stimulation is of the greatest importance. Early romantic attachments are common with Venus in Aries, so it is very important to establish a genuine sense of romantic continuity. Early marriage is not recommended, especially if it is based on sympathy. You may give your heart a little too readily on occasions.

Venus in Taurus

You are capable of very deep feelings and your emotions tend to last for a very long time. This makes you a trusting partner and lover, whose constancy is second to none. In life you are precise and careful and always try to do things the right way. Although this means an ordered life, which you are comfortable with, it can also lead you to be rather too fussy for your own good. Despite your pleasant nature, you are very fixed in your opinions and quite able to speak your mind. Others are attracted to you and historical astrologers·always quoted this position of Venus as being very fortunate in terms of marriage. However, if you find yourself involved in a failed relationship, it could take you a long time to trust again.

Venus in Gemini

As with all associations related to Gemini, you tend to be quite versatile, anxious for change and intelligent in your dealings with the world at large. You may gain money from more than one source but you are equally good at spending it. There is an inference here that you are a good communicator, via either the written or the spoken word, and you love to be in the company of interesting people. Always on the look-out for culture, you may also be very fond of music, and love to indulge the curious and cultured side of your nature. In romance you tend to have more than one relationship and could find yourself associated with someone who has previously been a friend or even a distant relative.

Venus in Cancer

You often stay close to home because you are very fond of family and enjoy many of your most treasured moments when you are with those you love. Being naturally sympathetic, you will always do anything you can to support those around you, even people you hardly know at all. This charitable side of your nature is your most noticeable trait and is one of the reasons why others are naturally so fond of you. Being receptive and in some cases even psychic, you can see through to the soul of most of those with whom you come into contact. You may not commence too many romantic attachments but when you do give your heart, it tends to be unconditionally.

Venus in Leo

It must become quickly obvious to almost anyone you meet that you are kind, sympathetic and yet determined enough to stand up for anyone or anything that is truly important to you. Bright and sunny, you warm the world with your natural enthusiasm and would rarely do anything to hurt those around you, or at least not intentionally. In romance you are ardent and sincere, though some may find your style just a little overpowering. Gains come through your contacts with other people and this could be especially true with regard to romance, for love and money often come hand in hand for those who were born with Venus in Leo. People claim to understand you, though you are more complex than you seem.

Venus in Virgo

Your nature could well be fairly quiet no matter what your Sun sign might be, though this fact often manifests itself as an inner peace and would not prevent you from being basically sociable. Some delays and even the odd disappointment in love cannot be ruled out with this planetary position, though it's a fact that you will usually find the happiness you look for in the end. Catapulting yourself into romantic entanglements that you know to be rather ill-advised is not sensible, and it would be better to wait before you committed yourself exclusively to any one person. It is the essence of your nature to serve the world at large and through doing so it is possible that you will attract money at some stage in your life.

Venus in Libra

Venus is very comfortable in Libra and bestows upon those people who have this planetary position a particular sort of kindness that is easy to recognise. This is a very good position for all sorts of friendships and also for romantic attachments that usually bring much joy into your life. Few individuals with Venus in Libra would avoid marriage and since you are capable of great depths of love, it is likely that you will find a contented personal life. You like to mix with people of integrity and intelligence but don't take kindly to scruffy surroundings or work that means getting your hands too dirty. Careful speculation, good business dealings and money through marriage all seem fairly likely.

Venus in Scorpio

You are quite open and tend to spend money quite freely, even on those occasions when you don't have very much. Although your intentions are always good, there are times when you get yourself in to the odd scrape and this can be particularly true when it comes to romance, which you may come to late or from a rather unexpected direction. Certainly you have the power to be happy and to make others contented on the way, but you find the odd stumbling block on your journey through life and it could seem that you have to work harder than those around you. As a result of this, you gain a much deeper understanding of the true value of personal happiness than many people ever do, and are likely to achieve true contentment in the end.

Venus in Sagittarius

You are lighthearted, cheerful and always able to see the funny side of any situation. These facts enhance your popularity, which is especially high with members of the opposite sex. You should never have to look too far to find romantic interest in your life, though it is just possible that you might be too willing to commit yourself before you are certain that the person in question is right for you. Part of the problem here extends to other areas of life too. The fact is that you like variety in everything and so can tire of situations that fail to offer it. All the same, if you choose wisely and learn to understand your restless side, then great happiness can be yours.

Venus in Capricorn

The most notable trait that comes from Venus in this position is that it makes you trustworthy and able to take on all sorts of responsibilities in life. People are instinctively fond of you and love you all the more because you are always ready to help those who are in any form of need. Social and business popularity can be yours and there is a magnetic quality to your nature that is particularly attractive in a romantic sense. Anyone who wants a partner for a lover, a spouse and a good friend too would almost certainly look in your direction. Constancy is the hallmark of your nature and unfaithfulness would go right against the grain. You might sometimes be a little too trusting.

Venus in Aquarius

This location of Venus offers a fondness for travel and a desire to try out something new at every possible opportunity. You are extremely easy to get along with and tend to have many friends from varied backgrounds, classes and inclinations. You like to live a distinct sort of life and gain a great deal from moving about, both in a career sense and with regard to your home. It is not out of the question that you could form a romantic attachment to someone who comes from far away or be attracted to a person of a distinctly artistic and original nature. What you cannot stand is jealousy, for you have friends of both sexes and would want to keep things that way.

Venus in Pisces

The first thing people tend to notice about you is your wonderful, warm smile. Being very charitable by nature you will do anything to help others, even if you don't know them well. Much of your life may be spent sorting out situations for other people, but it is very important to feel that you are living for yourself too. In the main, you remain cheerful, and tend to be quite attractive to members of the opposite sex. Where romantic attachments are concerned, you could be drawn to people who are significantly older or younger than yourself or to someone with a unique career or point of view. It might be best for you to avoid marrying whilst you are still very young.

AQUARIUS:
2008 DIARY PAGES

October
2008

1 WEDNESDAY ☿ *Moon Age Day 1 Moon Sign Libra*

The first day of October offers you scope to look towards your social life with renewed vigour and a determination to make things more exciting. You can't go for long at a time without pepping things up in one way or another, and today would be an ideal time to plan for a very special sort of happening at the weekend.

2 THURSDAY ☿ *Moon Age Day 2 Moon Sign Scorpio*

Today's influences are not of the best sort for clear-headed planning, and there might be occasions when you find yourself baffled by things that normally wouldn't confuse you at all. You need time out to resolve issues and shouldn't get so carried away with half a dozen jobs that you fail to do any one of them to the best of your ability.

3 FRIDAY ☿ *Moon Age Day 3 Moon Sign Scorpio*

Make the most of the good things happening around you, even if you are not directly involved in everything. When it comes to personal enjoyment you may decide to wait until the evening, particularly if you remain extremely busy from a practical point of view. Routines can seem extremely tedious at times and are best avoided.

4 SATURDAY ☿ *Moon Age Day 4 Moon Sign Sagittarius*

In terms of your personality you can dominate most proceedings across the weekend and that could start very early on today. Why not spend some time with friends if you can, and keep your day bright and breezy? This is probably not the right time for serious conversations or for trying to sort out the whys and wherefores of the world.

50

5 SUNDAY   ☿ *Moon Age Day 5 Moon Sign Sagittarius*

By all means keep plugging away at home, getting things the way you want them to be for the weeks and months ahead, but at the same time you need to please yourself socially too. You may not be at your most patient today, and casual attachments, together with instant and not too important happenings might suit you best.

6 MONDAY   ☿ *Moon Age Day 6 Moon Sign Sagittarius*

Trends assist any Aquarians who have been feeling slightly out of sorts across the last few days to feel a good deal better. There is certainly likely to be a more positive attitude available from the world at large, and some of those things you have wanted to do for a while but were restricted from completing are now possible.

7 TUESDAY   ☿ *Moon Age Day 7 Moon Sign Capricorn*

It's worth having a close look at any new moneymaking projects, because you can't dismiss everything without examination. Someone rather special might be coming into your life around this time, maybe a celebrity or a person you have worshipped from afar. What follows could be very interesting indeed.

8 WEDNESDAY   ☿ *Moon Age Day 8 Moon Sign Capricorn*

You can be intriguing and intrigued today – it's a two-way process. Almost anything can captivate your curiosity and imagination, and at the same time you have what it takes to fascinate others. What are you doing to engender these strange reactions? Nothing at all except being a fairly typical Aquarian subject.

9 THURSDAY   ☿ *Moon Age Day 9 Moon Sign Aquarius*

The lunar high offers one of the strong points of the month and will almost certainly allow you a greater sense of freedom, self-choice and potential success. It isn't as if money is being handed to you in buckets, but you do now have a greater sense of purpose and a really good ability to sniff out some genuine advantages.

10 FRIDAY ☿ *Moon Age Day 10 Moon Sign Aquarius*

You can continue to get things going well for you, and with an upturn in general fortunes comes an improvement in your mental attitude. What before seemed impossible now only appears slightly difficult and what used to be hard is now routine. Your mental capacity is especially well starred, and likely to remain so for much of this month.

11 SATURDAY ☿ *Moon Age Day 11 Moon Sign Aquarius*

For the third day in a row the Moon is in Aquarius, helping you to stay on top form. There may be some personal situations around today that you may want to avoid, probably by refusing to talk about them, but in the main you can make significant progress and ought to feel generally good with your lot in life.

12 SUNDAY ☿ *Moon Age Day 12 Moon Sign Pisces*

This could turn out to be one of the most progressive Sundays you will experience during the autumn. You have a greater than average capacity to keep going, well after others have fallen by the wayside. There are advantages on offer that you may not have previously suspected, but the important thing is that you react quickly.

13 MONDAY ☿ *Moon Age Day 13 Moon Sign Pisces*

A break from routine might be necessary this week, even if you are hedged around by the everyday necessities and responsibilities of life. How you can ring the changes and yet still do what is expected of you is going to be your homework for the first part of the week, but if anyone can find a way, Aquarius certainly can!

14 TUESDAY ☿ *Moon Age Day 14 Moon Sign Aries*

The general state of romance improves under present planetary trends and that helps you to find wonderful company and to say exactly the right things to deepen an existing attachment or to form one in the first place. You are rarely stuck for words, but just at present they should drip from your tongue like honey.

15 WEDNESDAY ☿   *Moon Age Day 15 Moon Sign Aries*

Some busy preparation is called for, and there may not be time to scratch your nose today if you want to make the very best of what is around you. If you are approaching the end of a particular task or sequence of jobs that has been going on for some time, why not get your head around what you are going to tackle next?

16 THURSDAY ☿   *Moon Age Day 16 Moon Sign Taurus*

It has to be said that there are times when a tried and tested approach is the best one to adopt, though you sometimes don't realise the fact. Everything in your life is change and originality – that's just the way you are. Nevertheless, if you don't follow an expected path today you could be brought firmly down to earth with a bump.

17 FRIDAY   *Moon Age Day 17 Moon Sign Taurus*

Romantic plans might have to be changed at short notice – not that this need bother you too much because you are used to thinking on your feet. It could be that you have blundered without realising, and so might have to make a few apologies before you can get your usual level of co-operation from others and from your lover especially.

18 SATURDAY   *Moon Age Day 18 Moon Sign Gemini*

Whilst others get all complicated about solving little problems, you can have them sorted in no time at all. This is the sort of behaviour that gets you noticed and especially so under present planetary trends. You barely have to open your mouth today before someone declares you to be a genius. It might not be true, but it is gratifying.

19 SUNDAY   *Moon Age Day 19 Moon Sign Gemini*

Be prepared to keep your ambitions under close scrutiny for the next few days. It isn't that you are any less potentially successful than you usually are, merely that you may be expecting rather too much, even of your skills. Things will go much smoother if you are willing to accept that there are some things you don't know. That might mean seeking help.

20 MONDAY
Moon Age Day 20 Moon Sign Cancer

Most noteworthy of all in your life just now is your creative potential. You should know instinctively what looks and feels right and can really wow people with your sense of style. Add to this a very positive attitude to life and an expression that says you can't believe everyone is not as cool as you are, and success is there for the taking.

21 TUESDAY
Moon Age Day 21 Moon Sign Cancer

Your strength today lies in doing everything you can to support the underdog. If there is one thing you cannot abide it is a bully or people who want to foist their redundant ideas onto everyone else. That's why if you see someone who looks downtrodden today, you can afford to leap to their defence.

22 WEDNESDAY
Moon Age Day 22 Moon Sign Leo

Certain aspects of material progress could be difficult whilst the lunar low is around, and you may not be half so cocksure of yourself as has been the case across the last few days. Nor will speaking out in company be your top priority – in fact it might be far more comfortable to spend as much time as possible on your own.

23 THURSDAY
Moon Age Day 23 Moon Sign Leo

There are no instant solutions around at the moment, and the fact that you can't conjure answers from thin air could really get on your nerves. Fortunately this should be a very temporary phase and one that can't endure much beyond today. Even by this evening you can get back to being much more like your usual self.

24 FRIDAY
Moon Age Day 24 Moon Sign Virgo

There might be very little happening as far as your major ambitions and desires are concerned, and if you are willing to put up with being in the doldrums that's the way things will stay. However, if you inject a little extra effort into your life, circumstances should start to work in your favour. It's all a case of intervening at just the right time.

25 SATURDAY
Moon Age Day 25 Moon Sign Virgo

Despite your constant need to alter things at the drop of a hat, it is the stable work patterns and normal actions that bring the greatest potential rewards for the moment. Now is the time to still that butterfly mind and leave some of your originality alone, at least during this weekend. Be receptive to good ideas from others.

26 SUNDAY
Moon Age Day 26 Moon Sign Virgo

If you are surrounded by people who are constantly crying wolf, that could make you rather unsettled. It would be best to look at the evidence in any situation yourself and to then make up your own mind rather than relying on the opinions of others. In matters of love an attentive approach works best.

27 MONDAY
Moon Age Day 27 Moon Sign Libra

Progress could be significantly slowed at the start of this working week but more because of the actions of other people than on account of anything you are saying or doing. All you can really do is show a degree of patience and to help out whenever it proves to be possible. Fortunately you can make sure your social life is anything but slow.

28 TUESDAY
Moon Age Day 28 Moon Sign Libra

Things continue to buzz in terms of the bearing you can have on life outside work. Some Aquarians might be making extended journeys around this time, and if you are one of them you could find things working out even better than you had hoped. Even if you are forced to stick around the same place, you can allow your imagination to travel.

29 WEDNESDAY
Moon Age Day 0 Moon Sign Scorpio

The focus is on a strong desire to agree with others and to find a way forward, even where there have been significant difficulties in the past. You might also be particularly good at pouring oil on troubled waters as far as friends are concerned, and can use this to play the honest broker as this week moves on towards its end.

30 THURSDAY
Moon Age Day 1 Moon Sign Scorpio

Even if you are now slightly less assertive than was the case earlier in the month, to compensate you can be extremely sensitive, and shouldn't have any problem coming to conclusions that are based on intuition. This puts you one step ahead in certain situations and you would be well advised to follow your instincts most of the time.

31 FRIDAY
Moon Age Day 2 Moon Sign Sagittarius

Confidence is still present, even if it sometimes feels as though you are walking a tightrope today. Above all your courage is emphasised, assisting you to face people and situations that have really unnerved you in the past. Even if you quake a little inside, you needn't betray the fact.

November
2008

1 SATURDAY
Moon Age Day 3 Moon Sign Sagittarius

Your personal life could seem vague and complex – that is if you choose to analyse it too much. If you can't resolve all romantic issues just now, maybe you should concentrate instead on less emotional attachments, sticking to friends who want nothing but your company. Don't allow life to get too confusing or awkward.

2 SUNDAY
Moon Age Day 4 Moon Sign Sagittarius

You have scope to capitalise on favourable financial trends. Part of you says that you are involved in pipedreams whilst your deeper reasoning tells you to go ahead. There is no harm in at least exploring these avenues – that is if you tangibly recognise them.

3 MONDAY
Moon Age Day 5 Moon Sign Capricorn

The positive financial influences continue this week, so you need to pay attention and get things right first time. It is also possible for you to benefit from effort you put in previously and as a result of opportunities you may have thought were lost and gone forever.

4 TUESDAY
Moon Age Day 6 Moon Sign Capricorn

Because you are so good to have around you may well be in great demand at the moment. This isn't just a social thing but can extend to other spheres of your life too. When it comes to making a decision that is going to have a bearing on where you will be around this time next year, you may need to make your mind up now.

5 WEDNESDAY
Moon Age Day 7 Moon Sign Aquarius

Things can go from fairly quiet to positively hectic today and you need to be on top form in order to benefit from everything that is on offer. Only an Aquarian would try to do so, but if things look inviting you may not be able to help yourself. Romance is especially well highlighted today, with new understandings developing for some.

6 THURSDAY
Moon Age Day 8 Moon Sign Aquarius

With little time to think things through, much of what you achieve today may be done on automatic pilot. Not that you are especially interested in everyday routines. On the contrary, it is towards the showy and brash side of life that you are encouraged to turn during the lunar high, and why not? Nobody said we have to be serious all the time.

7 FRIDAY
Moon Age Day 9 Moon Sign Aquarius

If ever there was a time to let yourself go and to shock a few people on the way, this is it. Lady Luck is almost certainly on your side and it shouldn't be remotely difficult to make the very best of impressions on practically everyone. For Aquarius the weekend can be started early, and there are fifty different kinds of fun on offer!

8 SATURDAY
Moon Age Day 10 Moon Sign Pisces

Saturday might seem positively pedestrian after the last few days, but in reality you are able to achieve a great deal and can afford to be quite cheerful in the way you go about it. A day to make the most of interactions with family members and also close friends.

9 SUNDAY
Moon Age Day 11 Moon Sign Pisces

You still have scope to be on good form and open to new suggestions and all manner of possibilities. If you are an Aquarian who does not work at the weekend, why not earmark a good part of today to do something radically different? Invitations from friends are well accented under present trends.

10 MONDAY
Moon Age Day 12 Moon Sign Aries

Even if most people are reliable, there may be the odd one or two who are not, and these are the types you have to watch out for at present. Aquarians are not usually the type to be duped, but there could be some very skilled operators around at the moment and they might even take you in. When it comes to getting on at work, be bold.

11 TUESDAY
Moon Age Day 13 Moon Sign Aries

The focus is now on your willingness to put yourself at the disposal of others, both inside and outside of work. Some Aquarians will now be thinking in terms of new interests or hobbies, and if you are one of them, you can afford to move away from the pedestrian and the normal, towards something truly expressive.

12 WEDNESDAY
Moon Age Day 14 Moon Sign Taurus

The time is right to get well on side with those who are on the up. You don't normally use others as a vehicle towards your own success but if their elevator is on the way you might as well hitch a ride. In any case you needn't be just a passenger if you have your own original ideas. These contribute to the lives of colleagues and friends, not just yours.

13 THURSDAY
Moon Age Day 15 Moon Sign Taurus

It is towards your home life that you are encouraged to look today and maybe until the coming weekend. If relatives are especially kind to you right now, suspicious as you are under present planetary trends, you might wonder just what it is they are after. You may be about to find out!

14 FRIDAY
Moon Age Day 16 Moon Sign Gemini

Getting the everyday chores done can seem quite boring today, that is unless you look at them differently. There is nobody better than you for seeking a degree of originality or for discovering methods of work that are interesting as well as useful. You can afford to go through life with a definite skip in your step and a song in your heart now.

15 SATURDAY
Moon Age Day 17 Moon Sign Gemini

It looks as though for a day or two at least you have scope to dispense with your usual idealism, in favour of practical common sense. That works well in most cases, but people who like and trust your nature might feel you have suddenly become much more cynical than usual. Remember the adage, 'moderation in all things'.

16 SUNDAY
Moon Age Day 18 Moon Sign Cancer

Stand by for potential misunderstandings, brought about by a combination of the present position of Mars and Mercury in your solar chart. You simply misconstrue what others are saying and might make silly mistakes at every turn. Don't be alarmed because you can make most of what happens humorous and not serious.

17 MONDAY
Moon Age Day 19 Moon Sign Cancer

When it comes to getting your own way you have a number of weapons in your personal armoury today. Number one is your wonderful nature, which exudes joy and encourages others at every turn. In addition, you can be quite persuasive now, and have what it takes to convince everyone that what you want is also their ideal.

18 TUESDAY
Moon Age Day 20 Moon Sign Leo

The lunar low might slow you down a little, but it needn't prevent the general momentum you have built up in your life as a whole. Don't let anyone lord it over you at present and be prepared to stick up for yourself, even if you are not absolutely sure of the ground upon which you stand. Support from others can be sought later.

19 WEDNESDAY
Moon Age Day 21 Moon Sign Leo

This probably isn't the best day of the month to be considering any sort of speculation. It isn't that you are being foolish or gambling too much, it's merely that fortune doesn't favour your efforts at this time. You can improve this side of your life dramatically by the end of the week, but for now it's worth keeping your money where it is.

20 THURSDAY   *Moon Age Day 22 Moon Sign Leo*

For the third day in a row you would be wise to be careful and not take unnecessary chances of any sort. Stand up for yourself by all means, but it might be best to stand in the middle of any queue and not at the front, where you will attract more attention. You may decide to watch and wait until tomorrow, when the Moon moves on.

21 FRIDAY   *Moon Age Day 23 Moon Sign Virgo*

What a contrast to yesterday. Now you can show yourself to be very assertive, and needn't take no for an answer with regard to anything you see as being important. Neither will you be in the market for an argument, because you can stamp on anyone's opposition long before it gets to any sort of fall out.

22 SATURDAY   *Moon Age Day 24 Moon Sign Virgo*

You can afford to remain fairly passionate about your ideals and opinions, but not so much that you will let this get in the way of seeking a carefree and easy-going sort of weekend. All the same some of your ideas may be contentious, and you can't expect to be flavour of the month when you wear your personal badges on your sleeve.

23 SUNDAY   *Moon Age Day 25 Moon Sign Libra*

Trends support a more reasonable approach, in which you are less inclined to force your ideas onto others. This has been a strange departure for you because although Aquarius is a great thinker and even an intellectual, it isn't normally your way to dominate situations or people. An apology might just be called for today.

24 MONDAY   *Moon Age Day 26 Moon Sign Libra*

Make sure that you pay attention today, because knowing what you are talking about can make all the difference to the eventual outcome of a number of different situations. It's worth spending some of your time today thinking up ways to make your partner or lover more comfortable, and showing your charitable side.

25 TUESDAY *Moon Age Day 27 Moon Sign Scorpio*

There isn't any doubt at present about how attractive you can make yourself to others. This could lead to the odd embarrassing situation, especially since you can be quite naïve on occasions. What you take for natural kindness and someone's warm disposition could turn out to be much more!

26 WEDNESDAY *Moon Age Day 28 Moon Sign Scorpio*

It's time to stamp your personality onto certain situations, only now you can do so in a truly Aquarian way, without being bossy about it. Whilst others flap around in the shallows of life you are willing to head to deeper water, and you are about as impressive in your actions as your positive and happy-go-lucky sign can be.

27 THURSDAY *Moon Age Day 29 Moon Sign Scorpio*

Your mental prowess deepens, and when it comes to thinking things through nobody could beat you today. Anything really odd could capture your interest and you may also show a great fondness for history or culture around this time. People see you as being particularly intelligent – which only goes to show how perceptive they are!

28 FRIDAY *Moon Age Day 0 Moon Sign Sagittarius*

Life should be filled with possibilities at the moment, even if there are also one or two small disappointments. These are likely to come from the direction of practical efforts, some of which might have to be repeated. That shouldn't bother you much because you need to know that everything you do has been undertaken well.

29 SATURDAY *Moon Age Day 1 Moon Sign Sagittarius*

Look out for those mechanical and electrical devices, all of which may seem to have a down on you today. It might be best not to interfere too much and to allow people who know better what they are doing to sort things out. Meanwhile you can think up newer and better ways to spoil your friends and to motivate your relatives.

30 SUNDAY *Moon Age Day 2 Moon Sign Capricorn*

A twelfth-house Moon offers a chance for a quieter sort of Sunday, though one that can also be serene and comfortable. Aquarius does have a fondness for luxury on occasions, and this could be your chance to put your feet up. If you insist on being active, it's worth doing something that proves to be mentally stimulating too.

December

2008

1 MONDAY
Moon Age Day 3 Moon Sign Capricorn

It's up to you today to put in that extra bit of effort that can really make a difference. The planets say right now that if you leave things alone, that's the way they will stay, whereas if you interfere with life a little, almost anything is possible. You needn't allow anyone to push you to the back of the queue today, either at work or socially.

2 TUESDAY
Moon Age Day 4 Moon Sign Capricorn

This is likely to be a potentially good day for love, though more of the dreamy, poetical sort than the forceful, caveman type. In some respects a quieter time works best, but sandwiched between some strong planetary aspects and the arrival of the Moon into the sign of Aquarius, that isn't going to be the case for very long.

3 WEDNESDAY
Moon Age Day 5 Moon Sign Aquarius

The lunar high for December comes early in the month and offers you more energy, greater know-how and a strong intuition. Today you can stretch time to such an extent that almost anything is possible. You can be especially co-operative at the moment, so some of your successes could well be shared with colleagues or friends.

4 THURSDAY
Moon Age Day 6 Moon Sign Aquarius

If things are still going your way, you may not want to slow things down at all. Not everyone has your staying power so there could be occasions when it will be necessary to go it alone, but even this is no real problem just now. You can afford to push your luck a little, but despite the Moon's position this is not a time for overt gambling.

5 FRIDAY
Moon Age Day 7 Moon Sign Pisces

If there is one thing you relish at the moment it's a challenge. You can capitalise on any opportunity to pit your wits against people you respect as being good competitors, and you can be especially fair in your attitude right now. Keep your ears open because even a casual conversation could carry important messages.

6 SATURDAY
Moon Age Day 8 Moon Sign Pisces

Not everyone might agree with you today, particularly in a domestic sense. That's why you may have to make some compromises at home this weekend. A fair approach works best, whether the disagreement is simple, or more serious.

7 SUNDAY
Moon Age Day 9 Moon Sign Pisces

OK, so this isn't the best part of the year as far as the weather is concerned but that needn't prevent you from having a good time. Winter can be quite depressing, especially when you know there are months of it to come, but right now you can be inventive and curious. Why not think of somewhere to go that is completely different?

8 MONDAY
Moon Age Day 10 Moon Sign Aries

If you want to make things happen in a concrete sense, this is the part of the month to get moving. There can be significant developments at work for some, whilst other Aquarians could be making changes to their social lives. In many respects it's off with the old and on with the new – which is always of interest to your zodiac sign.

9 TUESDAY
Moon Age Day 11 Moon Sign Aries

What a great time this is for entertaining the crowds. Your powers of communication have seldom been better and you are extremely confident about yourself and the bearing you can have on the lives of others. When you are not out in front of a crowd you can afford to be more contemplative and to look deep inside yourself.

10 WEDNESDAY   *Moon Age Day 12 Moon Sign Taurus*

This great balance between your outward-facing self and your
inward-looking qualities continues today, giving you everything you
need to think and act in a positive and yet thoughtful manner. You
can persuade practically everyone to like you at the moment,
though of course there are bound to be exceptions.

11 THURSDAY   *Moon Age Day 13 Moon Sign Taurus*

Look out for sudden opportunities to broaden your experience
base, and don't turn down invitations that seem exciting, even if
some of these unnerve you a little. You are both braver and more
intrepid than you sometimes think, and especially so at this stage of
December. People from the past may well feature in your life again.

12 FRIDAY   *Moon Age Day 14 Moon Sign Gemini*

Being an Aquarian and so therefore always busy, it might only just
have occurred to you that Christmas is just around the corner. Now
is the time to get cracking, particularly if there are lots of things that
need organising and maybe all those presents to buy. By all means
put in some effort, though you needn't panic just yet.

13 SATURDAY   *Moon Age Day 15 Moon Sign Gemini*

This may turn out to be the best day of the month for all mental
activities – everything from a simple crossword to an appearance on
a television quiz show! Of course the former is more likely than the
latter, but either way you will be fascinated by anything that taxes
your mind and which causes you to realise just how bright you are.

14 SUNDAY   *Moon Age Day 16 Moon Sign Cancer*

Standing up for yourself should be no problem now, though you
need to avoid defending yourself before you are even attacked. This
may not turn out to be the best family Sunday of the month,
particularly if everyone seems to have different ideas and won't
listen to yours – which of course are the best of all.

15 MONDAY
Moon Age Day 17 Moon Sign Cancer

Make the most of today as far as work and practical matters are concerned, because the two-day lunar low is coming along. If there is anything that needs doing as a matter of urgency, you can't really afford to leave it any longer, and if ever the adage 'strike whilst the iron is hot' was applicable to you, it is especially true now.

16 TUESDAY
Moon Age Day 18 Moon Sign Leo

Be prepared for a few disappointments, or at the very least for a short interlude when you might doubt your own capabilities. Actually there's nothing wrong with anything you are doing, it's simply that you may not have your accustomed confidence. The time is right to seek some reassurance from friends.

17 WEDNESDAY
Moon Age Day 19 Moon Sign Leo

This is not an ideal time to gamble. Instead it's worth taking periods out from the rat race. Aquarius has a very contemplative side to its nature and you need to recognise and use that fact whilst the Moon remains in Leo. Even the lunar low can be of significant use if the period and circumstances it brings are used to your advantage.

18 THURSDAY
Moon Age Day 20 Moon Sign Virgo

It might seem as though you are a long way from reaching some of your dreams, but that's just the residue of the lunar low causing you to be a little pessimistic. As today wears on you can afford to be more and more cheerful and quite willing to join in with the fun and games that others are creating. Your own efforts come later.

19 FRIDAY
Moon Age Day 21 Moon Sign Virgo

Frustration is possible at the moment if you sense that limitations are being placed upon you, and that could cause you to react. In discussions you could be slightly prickly, but in the main you manage to understand that not everyone thinks the same. If anything really annoys you today it is likely to be people who are selfish.

20 SATURDAY   *Moon Age Day 22 Moon Sign Libra*

The weekend could bring a further realisation that Christmas is close. Today offers an opportunity to dash about from one shop to another, or else to find that perfect Christmas tree, only to watch it shed all its needles on the carpet. Never mind, that's what the festive season is about, and you can make sure there are plenty of laughs.

21 SUNDAY   *Moon Age Day 23 Moon Sign Libra*

You can continue to be light-hearted and happy to fall in line with what your friends and especially your partner want to do. There is a strong sense of curiosity about you at the moment, and you not only want to know that things happen, but why they occur, which might mean a bit of digging. Your love life should be comfortable.

22 MONDAY   *Moon Age Day 24 Moon Sign Scorpio*

Be prepared to do whatever you have to at work so that you can relax across the holidays without worrying about professional matters. This would be an especially good day to mix business with pleasure and to show your colleagues just how much you appreciate them. It is, however, not an ideal time to overindulge.

23 TUESDAY   *Moon Age Day 25 Moon Sign Scorpio*

Only two days to go, and you may still be way behind with your final preparations. Does this really worry you? Things will happen whether you monitor them or not, and everyone will manage to have a good time, even without each little detail being perfect. It's time for Aquarius to relax, you just don't realise it yet.

24 WEDNESDAY   *Moon Age Day 26 Moon Sign Scorpio*

Christmas Eve offers a warm glow and a sense of nostalgia regarding the way things used to be. Of course they never really were much different, it's just what the festive season does to everyone. Make the most of a deep sense of family affection and a desire to express the way you feel, especially to your lover.

25 THURSDAY
Moon Age Day 27 Moon Sign Sagittarius

Today could bring you much that you expected but also something that will be a real surprise – and it may not be wrapped in paper and tied with a ribbon. Make the most of any chance to get out of the house, because if you are forced to stay in with the turkey and mistletoe all day you might be chewing the carpet by the evening!

26 FRIDAY
Moon Age Day 28 Moon Sign Sagittarius

Once again you need change and diversity, and no matter how much family members demand your attention you would be better off seeking the company of friends at some stage today. The trouble is that even if you remain active and enterprising, you may have little or no way to utilise this side of your nature whilst the Christmas period continues.

27 SATURDAY
Moon Age Day 0 Moon Sign Capricorn

Looking at your depleted finances is probably not the best thing to be doing at the moment, though you can probably find something interesting to do today that costs you little or nothing. Party hats and streamers can only excite you for so long, and what you definitely need right now is something that isn't concerned with eating.

28 SUNDAY
Moon Age Day 1 Moon Sign Capricorn

You can afford to feel slightly more relaxed today and more willing to go with the flow than seems to have been the case across the last few days. Be prepared to respond to the demands of others. However, on the whole you stand a good chance of enjoying this particular day.

29 MONDAY
Moon Age Day 2 Moon Sign Capricorn

You have what it takes to end the year on a very high note, but for today at least you can be more introspective but at least somewhat less restless than of late. Your mind tends to go back in time and you are bitten once again by the Christmas nostalgia bug. Why not get in touch with friends and relatives who live a long way off?

30 TUESDAY
Moon Age Day 3 Moon Sign Aquarius

What a fine way to end a year! The Moon is back in Aquarius and you should be up for just about anything. If you put in a little preparation ahead of tomorrow's celebrations, you should enjoy them all the more. Don't allow pointless rules and regulations to get in the way, because for the moment you can make things up as you go along.

31 WEDNESDAY
Moon Age Day 4 Moon Sign Aquarius

You continue to be on fine form, and could be the one dancing in the fountains by midnight. No matter what your age you are young at heart and therefore extremely good to have around. A year-end flutter could work out well for you, and it seems as though you can't put a foot wrong. Just don't let things get too out of hand.

AQUARIUS:
2009 DIARY PAGES

AQUARIUS:
2009 IN BRIEF

There is plenty to keep you occupied at the beginning of the year, including anything you were unable to do across the holidays. You should be in gear quite quickly for January and February and anxious to get on with new starts to coincide with the new year. Friends should be especially helpful and colleagues will have plenty of input too. Romance could be a little topsy-turvy but can soon be sorted. You will know instinctively how to do the right thing in a professional sense.

March and April should be reasonably smooth going, but you might not be entirely satisfied with your progress at first. You are likely to be sluggish in your reactions and slower to respond to changing circumstances. All the same it won't take you long to catch up with the field and then April offers new challenges and the possibility of achieving a longed-for objective. Concentrate on communicating as effectively as possible.

Along comes the early summer and with May and June you should really begin to get into your stride. Give yourself the time you need to sort out situations before you throw yourself into them because there is no rush and plenty of time to get things right. At work you are likely to be making a good impression and could be able to achieve advancement. At home you show yourself to be receptive and willing to share. Loved ones are likely to respond in kind and will be doing all they can to please you.

July and August are likely to be the months during which you will travel the most, either with regard to business or, more likely, simply because you need the change. If there are any problems at all during this time these are likely to occur because you haven't checked details or because you are rushing again. Aquarians who have been looking for a new attachment should focus their energies around now for maximum success.

The autumn might see things slowing down a little, at least at first. Both September and October require more concentration and a sense of purpose that is greater than earlier in the year. The rewards can be great and money matters should look especially good. Get away from routines when you can and maybe take a late holiday. Stand by later for some positive news regarding a close personal friend or a relative.

The last two months of the year, November and December, will find you active, enterprising and probably more relaxed. You know what you want from life and will have a good idea how to get it. Romance looks especially good, as do all relationships, particularly across the Christmas period. You will be able to use the festive season to your advantage in a number of ways. There is every chance that you will finish the year on a notable high.

29

January
2009

1 THURSDAY
Moon Age Day 5   Moon Sign Aquarius

The very start of the year is an excellent time for you. The Moon is in your own zodiac sign of Aquarius, assisting your efforts to socialise. Even if you are feeling slightly hung over, it's worth summoning up the energy to get out and about. Make the most of today by starting the year as you mean to go on.

2 FRIDAY
Moon Age Day 6   Moon Sign Pisces

This has potential to be a fairly exacting period when it comes to business. There is little doubt about what you want and you can demonstrate your zest and enthusiasm in your dealings with others. If you can persuade people to trust you at the moment, that allows you to push certain issues to a greater extent than you might have done before.

3 SATURDAY
Moon Age Day 7   Moon Sign Pisces

The Sun is presently in your solar twelfth house, and although other planetary positions indicate a fairly hectic period, there may be part of you that would be happy to retreat into yourself. This is particularly true in terms of your personal life, which offers you scope for a quieter interlude during which you can afford to remain somewhat reserved.

4 SUNDAY
Moon Age Day 8   Moon Sign Aries

There isn't much doubt that when it comes to any plans you have been laying down of late you now have an opportunity to work swiftly and efficiently to put them into practice. Important discussions with others are a possibility, even if you are still fairly reticent to talk about your deepest emotions. Today responds very well to variety.

73

5 MONDAY
Moon Age Day 9   Moon Sign Aries

At the start of the first full working week of the year there is much to be said for seeking out the company of people you haven't seen across the Christmas break and for putting yourself in the market for a little luxury of some sort. Why not check out the January sales and acquire something you would never be able to afford under normal circumstances?

6 TUESDAY
Moon Age Day 10   Moon Sign Taurus

Life is a game of two halves at the moment as far as you are concerned. Whilst planets such as Venus and Mercury encourage you to get out there and take part in all sorts of different activities, the Sun supports more home-based activity. You could even feel a little insecure on occasions, though you may not be able to work out why.

7 WEDNESDAY
Moon Age Day 11   Moon Sign Taurus

If there are intimate issues that you know need dealing with as soon as possible, today is an ideal time to talk about them and also to listen closely to what your partner has to say. From a business point of view progress may be difficult, and a little extra patience would be no bad thing if you have to deal with intransigent types.

8 THURSDAY
Moon Age Day 12   Moon Sign Gemini

Love life and social matters are more positively highlighted for a day or two as the Moon moves into Gemini. The focus is on spending quality time with those you love the most and showing off a little – something you may not have done much since the start of the year. Aquarius needs to be on display regularly and today offers that chance.

9 FRIDAY
Moon Age Day 13   Moon Sign Gemini

Activities at work should now prove to be more enjoyable, and slowly but surely you should be gaining speed in your life generally. However, there is a word of caution. Until the Sun moves away from your solar twelfth house in the last third of the month, care is still advisable regarding your financial resources, and holding back is the name of the game.

10 SATURDAY   *Moon Age Day 14   Moon Sign Cancer*

Even if your ambitions are driving you forward, you may not always know for sure what the destination is going to be. As a rule this is no problem to you – after all you are a child of Aquarius. Unfortunately for the moment there are going to be ifs and buts that don't normally occur. Still, there is no harm in showing a little caution now and again.

11 SUNDAY   *Moon Age Day 15   Moon Sign Cancer*

The accent is now upon social activities and the way you use your natural attractiveness to others. You shouldn't have any difficulty at all in bringing people round to your way of thinking, nor in attracting admirers. There is a great deal of potential information on offer now. All you have to do is sort it out.

12 MONDAY   ☿   *Moon Age Day 16   Moon Sign Leo*

A little extra caution would be wise for the next couple of days. The Moon has moved into Leo, which is your opposite zodiac sign. This brings the once-monthly period known as the lunar low. Don't throw caution to the wind until the middle of the week and be prepared to look at matters extremely carefully. This is not a time to sparkle.

13 TUESDAY   ☿   *Moon Age Day 17   Moon Sign Leo*

Everyday progress could be fairly slow, if you are actually moving at all. Still, you don't have to be racing ahead all the time and you can afford to allow others to take some of the strain for a little while. You could use today to catch up with people you don't see very often and make sure all your communications are up to date.

14 WEDNESDAY ☿   *Moon Age Day 18   Moon Sign Virgo*

It won't be very long before the time is right for getting rid of anything that has been getting in your way, and now that the lunar low is finished you have an opportunity to look at all the potential changes that stand before you. There are good reasons for optimism over the next few days, and that's all it takes for Aquarius to begin simmering.

15 THURSDAY ☿ *Moon Age Day 19   Moon Sign Virgo*

Although in some ways you might be happy to settle for a distinctly quiet social scene, in other situations you have what it takes to be the centre of attention and attraction. It's really a case of not knowing what you want for the moment, though times will change significantly in only a few more days. A day to keep a sense of proportion at work.

16 FRIDAY ☿ *Moon Age Day 20   Moon Sign Libra*

Trends suggest you might have very little patience with jobs that bore you today and will want to free yourself from any restrictions that seem to be holding you back. Bear in mind that some of these restrictions may be necessary, and a little extra care would be wise before you decide to break free, particularly if you don't know what you want afterwards.

17 SATURDAY ☿ *Moon Age Day 21   Moon Sign Libra*

Information you may well put to good use could be available from a friend, a colleague or even your partner. You can turn today into a very definite learning period and can use it to discover things that will be of great use to you in the weeks and months ahead. The time is definitely right to keep your eyes and ears open.

18 SUNDAY ☿ *Moon Age Day 22   Moon Sign Libra*

There's nothing wrong with putting big ideas on the shelf for just a little while longer and enjoying what life has to offer at a low-key level. You may decide to stay around your home today and to take advantage of a little midwinter comfort. Affairs of the heart are well accented for the moment. Try a roaring fire and a delicious meal!

19 MONDAY ☿ *Moon Age Day 23   Moon Sign Scorpio*

Professional developments are significant at the start of this week because it is only a couple of days before great changes will become possible. Taking the odd chance this week could lead to much more than you expect, and it looks as though you will soon have a chance to display the real Aquarius. Today is best for planning rather than acting.

20 TUESDAY ☿ *Moon Age Day 24   Moon Sign Scorpio*

Now you can ensure that everything looks different. The Sun moves into your solar first house, bringing one of the best potential periods of the year. You can now make a favourable impact on all sorts of people and get everything lining itself up for you. Much of this has to do with your own attitude, so make sure it is positive and happy.

21 WEDNESDAY ☿ *Moon Age Day 25   Moon Sign Sagittarius*

Capitalise on the positive responses you can gain in terms of your social life because this is a time when good things are possible as a result of the actions of friends and associates. It is towards your regular social group that you are encouraged to turn your attention now, but don't be afraid to allow newcomers to enliven your life too.

22 THURSDAY ☿ *Moon Age Day 26   Moon Sign Sagittarius*

Fortunate changes to your finances are possible, even if you don't exactly recognise these for what they are worth at first. Your creative potential is highlighted, as is your great desire to feed your intellect. Be prepared to glean important information, even from people you meet in the most casual of ways. It's simply a matter of listening carefully.

23 FRIDAY ☿ *Moon Age Day 27   Moon Sign Sagittarius*

Don't be moved by peculiar moods to do things that are actually very untypical for you. At the same time there may be plenty of people who think they know better than you do how your life ought to be lived. Although you won't want to be rude to anyone, it's up to you now to make it plain that you know best what is right for your life.

24 SATURDAY ☿ *Moon Age Day 28   Moon Sign Capricorn*

Problems could arise in the area of communication. This is definitely a time to address issues and to find solutions. While others are jumping around from foot to foot, you are the one who can come up with all the good ideas. If you decide to start a new regime now, you have everything you need to succeed – it's part of the planetary deal.

25 SUNDAY ☿ *Moon Age Day 29   Moon Sign Capricorn*

The focus for the moment is on luxury and your need to feel more than comfortable with your lot in life generally. Don't overlook any new financial possibilities and keep your eyes open for any bargains that are available. Remaining positive in all your dealings will be the best way of overcoming any unforced errors.

26 MONDAY ☿ *Moon Age Day 0   Moon Sign Aquarius*

The Moon now moves into your own zodiac sign of Aquarius and with it comes that period of the month known as the lunar high. You have everything to play for, and should use this as an opportunity to put in extra effort in order to get what you really want. In conversation you have what it takes to be joyful, interesting and very good to know.

27 TUESDAY ☿ *Moon Age Day 1   Moon Sign Aquarius*

This is the right period to put new ideas to the test and also to gain the backing of people who can help make some of your dreams come true. An easier path to your objectives is now there for the taking, and you should be sweeping away cobwebs at every turn. Today should also be extremely fortunate as far as your social life is concerned.

28 WEDNESDAY ☿ *Moon Age Day 2   Moon Sign Aquarius*

If there are practical issues to be addressed at this stage of the week, you still have what it takes to deal with these fully. There is now much less of a tendency for you to retreat into your own little world and you can afford to feel more and more confident with your abilities. Standard responses may not work, so why not be original?

29 THURSDAY ☿ *Moon Age Day 3   Moon Sign Pisces*

Make the most of a time of self-discovery and the chance to better yourself in a number of different ways. There are many alternative ways in which to present yourself, and you needn't be afraid to try them all at this juncture. You can best pep up your social life by doing something completely different and by making interesting new friends.

30 FRIDAY ☿ *Moon Age Day 4   Moon Sign Pisces*

There could be more than a little self-indulgence around today and you need to be just a little careful that you don't overdo things. You would be wise to avoid any sort of overconsumption at this time. As far as money is concerned, there is much to be said for spoiling yourself somewhat, but it's worth spending time seeking out bargains.

31 SATURDAY ☿ *Moon Age Day 5   Moon Sign Aries*

If you feel unsure about any commitment you are now expected to make, it would be sensible to indulge in a little negotiation before any hard and fast deal is made. You won't want to go back on your word later and neither do you wish to upset anyone. But what is the point of taking on something that is going to be a drag later?

February
2009

1 SUNDAY
Moon Age Day 6   Moon Sign Aries

You now have scope to be a really impressive creature in a social sense. Today is about seeking out stimulating company and surprising other people with your abilities. Now is the time to lay on the charisma with a trowel and to ensure that almost everything you do is theatrical and designed to wow others!

2 MONDAY
Moon Age Day 7   Moon Sign Taurus

You should define and then follow your own path as much as proves to be possible this week. There is now a real chance for growth in your life and rather less confusion around you than seems to have been the case during January. Be prepared to keep abreast of current news and views, especially at work, and let others know that you are around.

3 TUESDAY
Moon Age Day 8   Moon Sign Taurus

There are good reasons to share some time with your loved ones today, even if you are quite busy in a practical sense. There are ways and means of mixing business with pleasure and a real ability on your part to break down the barriers of doubt and potential worry. In other words, you should be feeling on top form.

4 WEDNESDAY
Moon Age Day 9   Moon Sign Taurus

Mercury is now in your solar twelfth house and although for a few days this supports a quieter Aquarius again, you can still concentrate very well on the job at hand. The emphasis is on seeing things through to their ultimate conclusions rather than fudging issues. When it comes to affairs of the heart, quiet but definite progress is now possible.

5 THURSDAY   *Moon Age Day 10   Moon Sign Gemini*

Romance and pleasure receive something of a boost today, and financial matters are also well accented. This is an ideal time to make the most of money you can gain from less than expected directions – even if the minute it arrives there are bills coming in that will take some of it away again!

6 FRIDAY   *Moon Age Day 11   Moon Sign Gemini*

You have good administrative ability, and can use it to organise not only your own life but also the lives of those around you. The assistance you can give colleagues who request it is what really makes the difference now. Once the evening comes along you have scope to make your best potential successes of the day, so why not get out and mix?

7 SATURDAY   *Moon Age Day 12   Moon Sign Cancer*

Trends offer you a time of extreme dynamism and an overriding sense of purpose. If those around you don't understand what you want or where you need to be, you may decide you need to go it alone. This is probably the best time of the month to start ambitious new projects and to let the world know who you are.

8 SUNDAY   *Moon Age Day 13   Moon Sign Cancer*

This is a time when your fortune could seem to decrease somewhat. The approaching lunar low is inclined to bring you down a little, though more so from tomorrow on. With strong supporting planets on all sides what counts most is your sense of purpose and your ability to deal with small irritating issues in a moment.

9 MONDAY   *Moon Age Day 14   Moon Sign Leo*

A little caution would be no bad thing at the start of this new working week, but even if there are clouds on the horizon at first you can soon dispel them. The fact is that despite the lunar low you may be firing on all cylinders and just raring to have a go at almost anything that is on offer. Capitalise on new incentives from colleagues and especially superiors.

10 TUESDAY
Moon Age Day 15   Moon Sign Leo

You may tend to expect slightly too much or to leave the starting line before the gun has been fired. Your best approach is to take your time because you need to be sure of your footing in everything you do. You have scope to enliven your day with unexpected events, particularly in relation to your social life and love life.

11 WEDNESDAY
Moon Age Day 16   Moon Sign Virgo

It goes without saying under present trends that you have to leave certain things where they belong, firmly in the past. It's time to move on, and also a good period for dumping things that are no longer of any use to you. You can create warm moments as far as your love life is concerned, as well as a new understanding with your partner.

12 THURSDAY
Moon Age Day 17   Moon Sign Virgo

This can be a very good day when it comes to exchanging ideas and getting to grips with any issues that have troubled you for a while. Pointless worries can now be left behind, leaving you with a chance to commit yourself more fully to the future than at any time so far this year. Beware a tendency to be slightly fussy about issues that don't matter.

13 FRIDAY
Moon Age Day 18   Moon Sign Libra

The spotlight is on the world of the imagination rather than on getting involved in real issues that look as though they could be difficult. It isn't that you are retreating from the world in a general sense because you might still be quite happy to socialise and to chat to others. You simply don't want to push hard.

14 SATURDAY
Moon Age Day 19   Moon Sign Libra

Your competitive instincts begin to strengthen across the weekend. This supports a desire not simply to take part, but to be the best. In sporting activities you would be wise to take care against niggling little injuries, which are always a possibility if you don't know when to stand back and let others score the goals.

15 SUNDAY   *Moon Age Day 20   Moon Sign Scorpio*

Venus has now entered your solar third house and this offers a pleasant period. Your best approach is to look towards a time when differences can be left behind and when you are able to look forward instead of back. Even casual conversations could help you to unearth facts you didn't know, which could make you feel much better about yourself.

16 MONDAY   *Moon Age Day 21   Moon Sign Scorpio*

It probably pays to look at new issues and to promote yourself more now. How can people know what you are worth when they don't even know you exist? It isn't like Aquarius to stand in the shadows, and everything around you suggests that the time is right to move out into the light. Being talked about should be a positive thing right now.

17 TUESDAY   *Moon Age Day 22   Moon Sign Scorpio*

The focus is on continuing to create a busy social life and finding plenty to do both inside and outside of work. Once again it becomes possible to mix business with pleasure, and to turn someone who was simply a colleague before into something more this week. A day to get on with personal projects and look for a little support.

18 WEDNESDAY   *Moon Age Day 23   Moon Sign Sagittarius*

With Mars now strong in your solar first house you may well come across rather more forcefully than you intend. Now is the time to pull your punches a little, especially when you are dealing with timid types. In matters of love you shouldn't be frightened to take the lead, and now have what it takes to knock someone completely off their feet.

19 THURSDAY   *Moon Age Day 24   Moon Sign Sagittarius*

Trends assist you to use your dynamic self-confidence today, and your powers of attraction should be going through the roof. This isn't simply a romantic response but can work at almost any level of your life. People generally like you, but as the days pass you can demonstrate just how popular it is possible for you to be. Keep plugging away at work.

20 FRIDAY   *Moon Age Day 25   Moon Sign Capricorn*

An ideal day to get new projects started and to identify the financial wherewithal to complete them quickly and efficiently. Rather than worrying about pointless details, your best approach is to get on with life as you know it should be lived. This is Aquarius at its best and you shouldn't let even a twelfth-house Moon get in your way.

21 SATURDAY   *Moon Age Day 26   Moon Sign Capricorn*

You needn't be tardy when it comes to voicing your opinions or when you need to show how positive you are capable of being. The fact is that if you can demonstrate your talents to other people, they should be more than willing to give you a chance. Routines are for the birds today, and are best left for other people to follow.

22 SUNDAY   *Moon Age Day 27   Moon Sign Capricorn*

There may be just one thing in your life that has to wait for another day before you can address it properly, which is why there could be a slight sense of frustration about today. Hold your nerve and don't push harder than you know is sensible. By tomorrow you can ensure that everything looks even better than it does at the moment.

23 MONDAY   *Moon Age Day 28   Moon Sign Aquarius*

A phase of high energy and extreme activity is on offer for most Aquarians. Even if life has held you back in the past, now you have renewed energy and a greater sense of purpose at your disposal. The lunar high can also offer benefits as far as your love life is concerned. It's time to forget about being shy and to communicate to the best of your ability.

24 TUESDAY   *Moon Age Day 29   Moon Sign Aquarius*

You have what it takes to make professional and personal progress and to fill most of today with positive activity. Be prepared to leave pointless exercises behind and avoid wasting any time on your way to specific destinations. This is a day which favours travel as much in a physical sense as inside your head.

25 WEDNESDAY   *Moon Age Day 0   Moon Sign Pisces*

Aside from any efforts you are making at the moment to realise certain economic goals, there are good reasons to take steps to improve your all-round sense of security. Almost anything can be achieved if you make the most of present influences, though it's also worth putting some time aside to show those closest to you how you really feel.

26 THURSDAY   *Moon Age Day 1   Moon Sign Pisces*

A day to use your quick mind and to trust those strong hunches that are a present hallmark of your nature. Aquarius almost always thinks on its feet, and even if there are people around who think you take too many chances, you needn't be afraid to push forward all the time. That's what breeds the excitement you so often crave.

27 FRIDAY   *Moon Age Day 2   Moon Sign Aries*

Your attitude to people who come new into your life around this time is what really makes the difference now. There could be some new friendships to be made, one or two of which might last a lifetime. With everything to play for at work, you are in a position to finish the working week with a flourish. Romantic possibilities are also favoured.

28 SATURDAY   *Moon Age Day 3   Moon Sign Aries*

Getting the finer things in life is part of what Aquarius is about. You love a little luxury and to be able to buy the very best sometimes. This being the case, today is an ideal opportunity to get your skates on and to be out there hustling. There may be bargains to be had, but you shouldn't be afraid to haggle.

28

March

2009

1 SUNDAY
Moon Age Day 4   Moon Sign Aries

On the first day of March you have a chance to make sure that your home life is better than ever. There are options to move around more under present planetary trends but for today at least you may decide to stay close to your own domain. If you can get things to fall into place nicely, you may be happy pottering around, doing what pleases you.

2 MONDAY
Moon Age Day 5   Moon Sign Taurus

Anything can happen at the start of this week and you really do need to keep your eye on the ball if you want to get the very most out of the day. If the people around you are busy, they may not have time to stop and talk too much. That shouldn't bother you a great deal because you have what it takes to be up there sparring with the best of them today.

3 TUESDAY
Moon Age Day 6   Moon Sign Taurus

You always function well in roles that require courage and the ability to confront others if it proves to be necessary. Knowing how to handle stress is also important, and your capabilities are especially highlighted at the moment. You needn't let any small disagreements bother you at all, particularly if you remain focused on your chosen objectives.

4 WEDNESDAY
Moon Age Day 7   Moon Sign Gemini

This is one of the best days of the month for showing people generally what a big personality you have, as well as a big heart. Any little kindnesses you show to those around you will probably not be forgotten, and you should be able to attract plenty of love and affection at this time. Seeking warmth and companionship is a natural aspect of life now.

5 THURSDAY   *Moon Age Day 8   Moon Sign Gemini*

A good time to make favourable business commitments is on offer, though money worries are a possibility. Your best approach is to sit down and work things out properly, in case you have made some sort of mistake or miscalculation. The planets are now generally on your side, so be prepared to make the most of their supportive influence.

6 FRIDAY   *Moon Age Day 9   Moon Sign Cancer*

With fiery Mars presently in your solar first house, this would be an ideal time to seek a challenge of some sort. Don't worry because life could well find you plenty to do and there shouldn't be any shortage of little adventures. If it seems that standard responses to others don't work at present, don't be afraid to be very original.

7 SATURDAY   *Moon Age Day 10   Moon Sign Cancer*

You can use today to achieve a boost to your finances and to ensure appropriate recognition for those you care about. In a general sense you have everything you need to get yourself noticed more and to reap the benefits of the favours you can elicit. Be prepared to leave time aside to be with family members and especially younger people.

8 SUNDAY   *Moon Age Day 11   Moon Sign Leo*

There's nothing wrong with leaving potentially serious problems alone for the moment if you are not in the right frame of mind. Who knows, by the time you get back to them they could have disappeared of their own accord. It may be somewhat hard to think constructively for the moment, and that is a legacy of the lunar low.

9 MONDAY   *Moon Age Day 12   Moon Sign Leo*

It's worth leaving aside any serious intention to get on with anything quickly, because it may be difficult to get things to work out today. You need to be steady in your approach to life and to check all details carefully. By tomorrow you can get things back to normal, but if you try to rush ahead right now you could well be in for some disappointments.

87

10 TUESDAY
Moon Age Day 13   Moon Sign Virgo

You are now capable of taking some tough decisions, not just for yourself but on account of other people too. If it's a case of 'more of the same' today, you could become quite bored, so a change in routines could work wonders. You are basically a fighter right now, and can use this trait to cut through to the core of issues.

11 WEDNESDAY
Moon Age Day 14   Moon Sign Virgo

A personal matter of some sort may put you on the defensive and certain feelings are likely to be very close to the surface. Ask yourself whether you are seeing conflict where none really exists – if so, why not stop and take stock? By the evening you should be back on form and can allow social encounters to bring you out of yourself.

12 THURSDAY
Moon Age Day 15   Moon Sign Libra

This is an ideal time to focus at least part of your thinking on business opportunities. The Sun is now in your solar second house, assisting you to show a practical approach to life through which you can make sure things are being done in the way you think they should be undertaken. This can enhance your ability when it comes to handing out instructions.

13 FRIDAY
Moon Age Day 16   Moon Sign Libra

You can afford to feel happier and more confident today, and this should help you to avoid flying off the handle if things go wrong. A relaxed approach works best in your dealings with life generally, and there are gains to be made if you seek out people who are fun to have around you. A day to make full use of your normal Aquarian popularity!

14 SATURDAY
Moon Age Day 17   Moon Sign Libra

There could be some impatience when it comes to personal restrictions, especially if you feel that you are being held back without any real justification. Being anxious to get ahead is all very well, though you need to avoid making complications for yourself on the way. If others seem to be playing strange games, your best response is not to get involved.

15 SUNDAY   *Moon Age Day 18   Moon Sign Scorpio*

This is another advantageous period for practical investments, which are as likely to be related to the time you put in than to the money. You have scope to use your intuition and foresight to help out family and friends, and to get them to follow your lead. There are good romantic prospects for today and great fun to be had for those willing to pursue it.

16 MONDAY   *Moon Age Day 19   Moon Sign Scorpio*

Don't be afraid to get involved in things today, even if it means spending a little money. Business opportunities may well be available, some of them from fairly unexpected directions. Conforming to the expectations of other people may not always be too easy, so it's time to make sure that the unique side of your nature is now fully on display.

17 TUESDAY   *Moon Age Day 20   Moon Sign Sagittarius*

If you surround yourself with friends you can derive great contentment from their company. Don't be surprised at the help you can gain from others, and the fact that they might work on your behalf even when you have not asked them to do so. Getting others to take the initiative could offer you the chance to find time for relaxation.

18 WEDNESDAY *Moon Age Day 21   Moon Sign Sagittarius*

Money matters are back to the fore again, as they have been for a week or two now. If you feel as if you have been working long and hard to achieve your objectives and to get your reward, now is the time to really make things start to come together. Even if your partner is demanding more of your time, you needn't let that worry you.

19 THURSDAY   *Moon Age Day 22   Moon Sign Capricorn*

For the moment the Sun remains in your second house, encouraging you to continue to focus your mind on material considerations. In a day or two that could well alter, but current trends support a pedantic approach and an unwillingness to let anyone else interfere in your life. Much of this is atypical for Aquarius.

20 FRIDAY *Moon Age Day 23   Moon Sign Capricorn*

Although you need to be quite careful who you listen to today, there may well be people around who know exactly how to point you in the right direction. The problem is knowing when the information is reliable. Turn up your intuition to full and, if necessary, take a leap in the dark. Be confident in the accuracy of your hunches at this time.

21 SATURDAY *Moon Age Day 24   Moon Sign Capricorn*

Even if there isn't much in the way of difficulty to be faced today, you may decide to take a defensive approach in which you are reluctant to co-operate to the extent you usually would. As the day wears it's worth taking a more positive view about most things and by the evening you have what it takes to get more or less back to your usual self.

22 SUNDAY *Moon Age Day 25   Moon Sign Aquarius*

This is a really good day to solve problems and to keep in touch with everyone around you. Not only is the lunar high present, the Sun has now moved into your solar third house, which is excellent for all forms of communication. The more you talk, the more you also have scope to listen, and it is through this combination that you have a chance to prosper.

23 MONDAY *Moon Age Day 26   Moon Sign Aquarius*

Breakthroughs you can achieve in your career could open up entirely new vistas for you and allow you to feel much more contented with your lot than has been the case for the last couple of weeks at least. If there are big decisions to be made, you could hardly choose a better time for making them than that presented by current planetary trends.

24 TUESDAY *Moon Age Day 27   Moon Sign Pisces*

Your thinking, talking and general powers of instinctive understanding are well marked, and this is a time when you can afford to take some far-reaching decisions. You needn't be held back by details and should be quite happy to go with the flow regarding any issues that have worried you a lot before. Why not spend time with your family?

25 WEDNESDAY   *Moon Age Day 28   Moon Sign Pisces*

It may be time to look at the state of your finances again, but this time with a great deal more optimism and less of a tendency to worry than was evident last week. Now you should be able to see your way forward clearly in a number of different ways and you have what it takes to convince others that your plans are sound. People 'want' to listen to you.

26 THURSDAY   *Moon Age Day 0   Moon Sign Pisces*

Today works best if you avoid unnecessary distractions and where possible try to cut to the chase. By concentrating you are going to make a better job of almost anything, and you have a chance to impress others with your sheer professionalism. There isn't any doubt about your leadership qualities, and getting people to fall in line is the order of the day.

27 FRIDAY   *Moon Age Day 1   Moon Sign Aries*

Not only the Sun but now also Mercury is in your solar third house, which makes this the best time of the month, and probably the year, for communicating with others. Your chameleon-like ability to change with different circumstances and people should be much in evidence, assisting you to avoid getting off on the wrong foot with anyone at all.

28 SATURDAY   *Moon Age Day 2   Moon Sign Aries*

A day to catch up on news and views and to keep on talking. The weekend could well prove inspirational for you and there should be opportunities to break routines and to do things that are simply interesting for their own sake. Everything you learn comes in handy at some stage, which is something Aquarius tends to realise instinctively.

29 SUNDAY   *Moon Age Day 3   Moon Sign Taurus*

Intuition is strong and so is your capacity for affection. There should be few obstacles in your way at the moment, and you can turn this into the sort of Sunday on which you can please yourself and also make those around you happy. In the main you can afford to be relaxed and once again open to new experiences, places, and of course people.

30 MONDAY   *Moon Age Day 4   Moon Sign Taurus*

Trends encourage a jovial attitude at the start of this working week, though you may also be quite competitive. Although you can avoid getting frustrated or losing your temper, you won't want to be beaten at anything. Even apparently unimportant situations can bring out this competitive streak, but bear in mind its effect on more timid types.

31 TUESDAY   *Moon Age Day 5   Moon Sign Gemini*

You can afford to remain happy, optimistic and generous. Any artistic effort you put in today should pay dividends, and it is clear that you just know what looks and feels right. You can capitalise on this interlude by presenting yourself positively to the world and using your charms to their full effect.

29

April

2009

1 WEDNESDAY
Moon Age Day 6   Moon Sign Gemini

It's the first day of a new month and April will find no fools as far as Aquarius is concerned. All the same, if you are in the mood to be mischievous, the odd prank isn't out of the question. Even if people who enter your life at this time don't appear to be exactly your cup of tea, you have what it takes to alter that in just a short time.

2 THURSDAY
Moon Age Day 7   Moon Sign Cancer

Trends indicate a period of mental restlessness, as natural curiosity gives way to an almost panicky desire to know things. Remember that searching frantically for objects often results in many of them remaining hidden! The more relaxed you are, the greater is the chance that you can now get everything to fall into place.

3 FRIDAY
Moon Age Day 8   Moon Sign Cancer

Good communication is the cornerstone of potential success right now. Even if you are still somewhat restless and fidgety, the more you keep in touch with those around you, the greater is the chance that you can achieve relaxation. There's nothing wrong with seeking agreement and confirmation of your ideas from family members.

4 SATURDAY
Moon Age Day 9   Moon Sign Leo

The Moon is back in Leo, which means the arrival of the lunar low. Although this may restrict you in some ways, there is such a planetary combination in your solar third house that you have what it takes to remain happy and communicative. It's possible that not everything will go your way though, particularly in terms of travel arrangements.

5 SUNDAY   *Moon Age Day 10   Moon Sign Leo*

If you try to avoid commitment today you could get yourself in trouble with your partner. However, if you take control entirely you may be accused of interference. It's a fine line to walk, but if anyone can manage it, you can. Be prepared to ignore delays and disappointments and find ways to enjoy yourself without the need for prior planning.

6 MONDAY   *Moon Age Day 11   Moon Sign Virgo*

You may decide that the best response to restlessness today is to seek out some change and variety. Part of this is thanks to the position of Mercury, which also supports a sense of uncertainty regarding some situations. None of this should prevent you from showing yourself at your best, especially if you know that people are watching you.

7 TUESDAY   *Moon Age Day 12   Moon Sign Virgo*

Working your way towards a greater sense of financial security should be a natural aspect of life at the moment. There is much to be said for spending a little to make more later. Whether or not you can get family members to be more careful with cash remains to be seen, and a sense of frustration cannot be ruled out.

8 WEDNESDAY   *Moon Age Day 13   Moon Sign Virgo*

There are gains to be made by remaining mentally active during most of today and by seeking out new challenges that tax your intellect and which keep you busy. There should not be anything particularly difficult about the practical side of life, though a bit of extra diplomacy would be no bad thing in any dealings with loved ones.

9 THURSDAY   *Moon Age Day 14   Moon Sign Libra*

Now is the time to capitalise on your ability to experiment and to come up with new ideas, particularly where your work life is concerned. Unforced errors are also possible, but in the main if these come along your best response is simply to shrug your shoulders and try again. A day to let your originality shine, and to get yourself noticed!

10 FRIDAY
Moon Age Day 15   Moon Sign Libra

It looks as though you will be in a good position to call the shots and to persuade others that your way of doing things is probably the best for everyone concerned. This may not be universally the case and, as has been possible all week, there may be one or two people around who won't fall in line with your thinking, no matter what.

11 SATURDAY
Moon Age Day 16   Moon Sign Scorpio

You can now afford to be fairly optimistic and self-assured on those occasions when it matters the most. The weekend should give you the chance to think things through without being bothered too much by trivial details. However, some restlessness is possible, so don't be afraid to move around a good deal in one way or another.

12 SUNDAY
Moon Age Day 17   Moon Sign Scorpio

Issues of economic security could take on a certain urgency, and there is much to be said for overcoming what you see as being any weakness in this area of your life. You would be wise to avoid too much self-indulgence today. Too much of a good thing is definitely not an advantage to the average Aquarian.

13 MONDAY
Moon Age Day 18   Moon Sign Sagittarius

Social matters have potential to be fairly vibrant this week, and there will be every opportunity to get yourself better known in specific circles. The impression is that wherever you were on the back row of life, you now have what it takes to move to the front. That shouldn't bother you in the slightest, because there are advantages in being on display.

14 TUESDAY
Moon Age Day 19   Moon Sign Sagittarius

In practical matters a freelance approach may now work best. If you have to work with others, it's worth trying to get them to do things your way, though on occasions this may not be too easy. It is possible that you might be seen as a troublemaker in some circles, particularly if you are determined to upset the applecart on occasions.

15 WEDNESDAY   *Moon Age Day 20   Moon Sign Sagittarius*

As the Moon moves towards your twelfth house, you could feel as though things are getting a little sluggish. If this goes against the grain for you right now, one option is to try to speed up your life in some way. Whether or not this strategy will work remains to be seen, but don't be surprised if you just cause unnecessary confusion.

16 THURSDAY   *Moon Age Day 21   Moon Sign Capricorn*

Prepare to capitalise on some good ideas on the monetary front, though a measured and thorough approach works best in relation to life generally. Even if you can't make this the most exciting or inspiring day you will experience this month, you can still make the most of its advantages. Many of these come about as a result of the attitude of others.

17 FRIDAY   *Moon Age Day 22   Moon Sign Capricorn*

The emphasis now is on improving your life in every way possible. Putting your talents clearly on display will assist you to get yourself noticed where it matters the most. A day to avoid arguments, either at work or in a family sense. The more you are able to see eye-to-eye with those around you, the greater is the chance that they will follow your lead.

18 SATURDAY   *Moon Age Day 23   Moon Sign Aquarius*

There should be more than an element of luck to support you whilst the lunar high is present, and you need to take advantage of situations that go your way. Following up on things is vitally important, so no laziness is allowed at the moment. New career openings are possible for some, whilst all Aquarians have scope to find contentment at home.

19 SUNDAY   *Moon Age Day 24   Moon Sign Aquarius*

This has potential to be a time of great excitement and very interesting possibilities. You won't get the full force of the lunar high if you stick around your house all day, and there is no doubt that the best possibilities arise when you are out and about. Personal ambitions count for a great deal, so why not persuade friends to help you realise some of them?

20 MONDAY
Moon Age Day 25   Moon Sign Aquarius

For the first part of today at least the lunar high is still around, assisting you to make this a fairly breakneck start to the week. Advantages are available from being in the right place at the right time, and even if some people are reticent to do anything much, your own level of progress remains high and you can make things happen.

21 TUESDAY
Moon Age Day 26   Moon Sign Pisces

Trends encourage you to focus on domestic and family issues for the next few weeks and this is because the Sun has now moved on to your solar fourth house. Of course you needn't allow yourself to be tied up with such thoughts all the time, but there's nothing wrong with being more concerned than usual for those with whom you live.

22 WEDNESDAY
Moon Age Day 27   Moon Sign Pisces

It pays to economise for a day or two because it might be all too easy to spend money needlessly under present trends. You have scope to get real value for money if you look around, and there should be some bargains to be had. This is not a time to let rules and regulations get on your nerves, and a relaxed approach is your best response.

23 THURSDAY
Moon Age Day 28   Moon Sign Aries

Peace and quiet may be difficult to find at home. The focus is on communication – it might feel as if everyone wants to talk at once, and they all want to talk to you! Make the most of today by enjoying the cut and thrust of family life and the fact that you are needed by others. Ask yourself whether complaining about the racket will do any good.

24 FRIDAY
Moon Age Day 29   Moon Sign Aries

Domestic activities offer the chance to achieve a greater degree of contentment, and even if you have the opportunity to be away from home you may decide not to take it. Although you are in a phase when you can gain greatly from peace and quiet, what actually matters the most is that you feel secure and loved by your immediate circle.

25 SATURDAY *Moon Age Day 0   Moon Sign Taurus*

Your strength lies in your ability to be expressive and to communicate well across the board. Of course there is nothing new about this for Aquarius, but you might be even chattier than usual. With many different interests on offer it shouldn't be hard to fill your Saturday, and the evening offers you scope to be socially motivated and full of beans!

26 SUNDAY *Moon Age Day 1   Moon Sign Taurus*

A brisker day is on offer, and one that gives you an opportunity to fulfil your responsibilities while remaining on the move. Even if you are dashing about, it would be sensible to keep your eyes and ears open because there is useful new input available all the time. Avoid forcing your opinions on others – they probably won't appreciate it.

27 MONDAY *Moon Age Day 2   Moon Sign Gemini*

The start of a new week works best if you make every effort to split your time between work and the necessary demands that surround you at home. You might feel these more keenly because of the present position of the Sun, but remember that other people can do things too, and you need to encourage everyone to pull their weight this week.

28 TUESDAY *Moon Age Day 3   Moon Sign Gemini*

Make the most of today by seeking out the company of interesting people and the chance to put forward your own thoughts in congenial surroundings. A good meal in the company of fascinating folk might suit you down to the ground, and even if this is impossible during the week there's nothing to stop you arranging something for another day.

29 WEDNESDAY *Moon Age Day 4   Moon Sign Cancer*

This would be an ideal time for forward planning and for getting to grips with anything that has been a mystery to you in the past. In most situations you have what it takes to be patient and determined and to do all you can to consolidate your position. Aquarius can be extremely shrewd at the moment, and you needn't let anyone fool you.

30 THURSDAY   *Moon Age Day 5   Moon Sign Cancer*

Perhaps the time is right for some change as far as your usual routines are concerned, and you may even decide to turn the normal events of family life upside down. At work there are gains to be made from being in the right place to influence colleagues, and there's always a chance that you are being carefully assessed at present.

 28

May

2009

1 FRIDAY
Moon Age Day 6   Moon Sign Cancer

The best way to influence the world at the start of May is by being ready to alter your attitude and your actions at a moment's notice. It is the very adaptability of Aquarius that proves to be its best ally, and this is certainly going to be the case right now. Today could be far more inspiring than the weekend ahead is likely to be.

2 SATURDAY
Moon Age Day 7   Moon Sign Leo

The lunar low is around during the weekend, and this might take the wind out of your sails in some respects. From a social point of view you can still be on top form, though you may not have your usual amount of energy and will gain from short periods of rest. Keep stimulating your mind because you need to feel challenged.

3 SUNDAY
Moon Age Day 8   Moon Sign Leo

Today offers great scope for thinking, but is not an especially fortunate time for doing too much. Bear in mind that if you take on anything too complicated, you may have to do it again, particularly if you are not as dextrous as would usually be the case. A day to concentrate on personal attachments and enjoy giving and receiving compliments.

4 MONDAY
Moon Age Day 9   Moon Sign Virgo

You should now be at your best when you are amongst close friends or at the very least with people you know are fond of you. Don't be in the least surprised if you discover you have an admirer you didn't know about, particularly if you are displaying your charms to the full at the moment. This should be a good week to shine romantically.

5 TUESDAY   *Moon Age Day 10   Moon Sign Virgo*

Right now a change of scenery might do a great deal to lighten your load in life, and working all the time is not an ideal situation. The odd break encourages you to commit yourself more when you are applying yourself, and also gives you a chance to develop your ideas. Personal freedom is particularly important to Aquarius at present.

6 WEDNESDAY   *Moon Age Day 11   Moon Sign Libra*

You would be wise to avoid getting into unnecessary and pointless discussions with others. There is nothing wrong with disagreeing, but this could so easily turn into an argument – and do you have the time to be at odds with people? Be prepared to help others with practical matters, especially if they are trying to do something you are very good at.

7 THURSDAY   ☿   *Moon Age Day 12   Moon Sign Libra*

You can afford to enjoy the sort of company you are keeping at the moment and to feel quite liberated by your social contacts. At the same time your mind may be inclined to focus on the past, often when you least expect it. Dreams could take you straight back to someone who was once extremely significant in your life.

8 FRIDAY   ☿   *Moon Age Day 13   Moon Sign Scorpio*

There isn't much doubt about your ability to charm people under present planetary trends. Aquarius can be warm and sociable at the best of times, but if you now turn the charisma up to full you can gain even more admirers as a result. Even if you don't mean to give someone the 'come on', bear in mind that that could be the way it seems to them.

9 SATURDAY   ☿   *Moon Age Day 14   Moon Sign Scorpio*

Today could be quite sluggish professionally, and so probably works out better for those Aquarians who do not have to work at the weekend. From a social point of view you should be on top form, and can take this opportunity to mix with people you find as outgoing and cheerful as you presently are. Ask yourself whether all your friends are happy now.

10 SUNDAY ☿ *Moon Age Day 15   Moon Sign Scorpio*

The Moon offers a boost to all friendships and team efforts. Your ability to co-operate has rarely been better, and you can use it to get everyone to do exactly what you want them to do, though without them even being aware of the fact. Stand by to take advantage of a day of rather strange but very positive coincidences and a great deal of intuition.

11 MONDAY ☿ *Moon Age Day 16   Moon Sign Sagittarius*

If you decide to take on new situations, you need to be especially careful to be diplomatic with others. Even if you know what you are doing, those around you may not, which is why you have to show as much patience as you can muster. Remember that particularly sensitive types could be somewhat put off by your present up-front style.

12 TUESDAY ☿ *Moon Age Day 17   Moon Sign Sagittarius*

Intimate matters can now take centre stage in your life, and you can use this as an opportunity to sort something out relating to your love life. There's nothing wrong with attracting attention from a number of different directions, nor with impressing people at work. This is Aquarius at its best, but you do need to slow down from time to time.

13 WEDNESDAY ☿ *Moon Age Day 18   Moon Sign Capricorn*

Mercury is still in a good position to help you to enliven your personal life and also to turn social events into something quite special. There might not be quite as much time as you would wish to discuss things with colleagues, and even at home you may well feel that you are constantly 'dashing through' and that you have few moments for gossip.

14 THURSDAY ☿ *Moon Age Day 19   Moon Sign Capricorn*

The Moon is now in your solar twelfth house, and taken together with what is happening elsewhere in your chart this could lead to some slight mental confusion. You need to be especially careful about arrangements and to make sure that if you have committed yourself to something you can be guaranteed to actually turn up.

15 FRIDAY
☿ *Moon Age Day 20*   *Moon Sign Capricorn*

You still may not feel yourself to be on top from, and it is entirely possible that you will be getting things wrong that you usually deal with easily. Why not enlist the support of your friends and of course colleagues at work? Beware of allowing people you don't see too often to dominate your thoughts at this time.

16 SATURDAY
☿ *Moon Age Day 21*   *Moon Sign Aquarius*

Like pushing a button you can dispel the confusion and emerge into the bright sunshine of potential success. The lunar high comes along just as the weekend gets going, and it offers you opportunities for new starts and fresh vistas. You can afford to feel very good about yourself today and tomorrow, and can make gains just by being who you are.

17 SUNDAY
☿ *Moon Age Day 22*   *Moon Sign Aquarius*

An ideal day to look for something bigger, better and brighter. A fast pace of events can work well in your social life, and you can also capitalise on the good luck that is generally available. There are potential gains to be made from being in the right place to profit from random chance, and you need to ask yourself whether it really is random at all.

18 MONDAY
☿   *Moon Age Day 23*   *Moon Sign Pisces*

Unexpected ups and downs are possible at the start of this week, some of which may be linked to the actions of friends and colleagues. Even if you don't want to be an especially deep thinker at the moment, that shouldn't stop you keeping the needs of people you care for in mind. This is the best way of ensuring you receive affection in return.

19 TUESDAY
☿   *Moon Age Day 24*   *Moon Sign Pisces*

Positive family trends are now underlined in your solar chart. This is a time when you have scope to enjoy having relatives around you, though your relationship with your partner is the key one at present. New understandings become possible, as well as a closeness that even eclipses what has gone before. Prepare to address the demands of friends.

20 WEDNESDAY ☿   *Moon Age Day 25   Moon Sign Aries*

You could find yourself at odds with others over situations that normally wouldn't occur to you at all. Even if you don't insist on having your own way, perhaps those around you are determined to be obstructive. Ignore these trends because you can be busy in other ways, and probably won't have too much time to pick over the bones of irrelevancies.

21 THURSDAY ☿   *Moon Age Day 26   Moon Sign Aries*

You are now at your very best with communication and all fresh ideas. There are chances to find new ways to do things and to create a sort of enchantment that you should relish. Your mind sometimes works in a peculiar way, which might make others think you are a little odd. At the end of the day, there's nothing wrong with being different.

22 FRIDAY ☿   *Moon Age Day 27   Moon Sign Aries*

Romance should now be your forte. Once again your mind is encouraged to go back to a past love or to the way you once viewed a much lower-key relationship. Maybe you are trying to recapture the past, but for Aquarius that just isn't possible. It is far better to commit yourself to whatever is happening around you right now.

23 SATURDAY ☿   *Moon Age Day 28   Moon Sign Taurus*

You can now afford to be more receptive to family members and to your partner. Even if you aren't short of something to do at the moment, it's worth finding time to stand and stare now and again. Enjoying the early summer weather would be no bad thing, and getting out and about can work wonders.

24 SUNDAY ☿   *Moon Age Day 0   Moon Sign Taurus*

Avoid making snap decisions for a day or two. Any tendency to make up your mind instantly is best put to one side, since this may not be such a good idea at this juncture. The more you analyse things, the greater is the likelihood that you will get them right first time. New educational opportunities are well marked for Aquarius.

25 MONDAY ☿ *Moon Age Day 1   Moon Sign Gemini*

The Sun is now in your solar fifth house, offering you a tremendous boost to love and romance generally. You are in a position to capitalise on your continuing popularity. Today is also ideal for putting right any misunderstandings, even those that go back for months or even years.

26 TUESDAY ☿ *Moon Age Day 2   Moon Sign Gemini*

You should be able to put your persuasive powers to good use when it comes to bringing others round to your specific point of view. If those around you seem to be engaged in some sort of spring-clean, it might occur to you that the time is right to dump things that are no longer of any practical use to you.

27 WEDNESDAY ☿ *Moon Age Day 3   Moon Sign Cancer*

Today could prove to be quite satisfying from a domestic point of view, though progress in practical matters might be a different story. You need to give life a significant kick up the backside, and even if this doesn't go down well with everyone, it might at least prevent an impasse from developing and keep things jogging along well.

28 THURSDAY ☿ *Moon Age Day 4   Moon Sign Cancer*

The focus is on your heightened creativity at the moment, and you may decide to turn some of this in the direction of your home. You know instinctively what looks and feels right and needn't take no for an answer when you have made up your mind regarding a specific change. You can afford to be fairly stubborn at the moment.

29 FRIDAY ☿ *Moon Age Day 5   Moon Sign Leo*

The changes go on, but some of them leave you behind for the next couple of days as the lunar low heralds a potentially quieter time when you may choose to retreat into your own little world. Be prepared to deal with hold ups and the need to reorganise your plans at the last minute. A cheerful approach is likely to work best.

30 SATURDAY ☿ *Moon Age Day 6 Moon Sign Leo*

Circumstances may still seem to be working against you, and the fact is that you need to be quite circumspect in the way you approach life generally. Not everyone that looks unfortunate turns out to be so at all. Disasters are unlikely, though some genuine embarrassment is possible as a result of something you do quite innocently.

31 SUNDAY ☿ *Moon Age Day 7 Moon Sign Virgo*

Emotional support is there for the taking and now that the lunar low is out of the way you have what it takes to speed towards your various destinations once more. You could be late getting started with important projects, but if you have taken your time during the last couple of days, you can use this to work to your advantage now.

29
June
2009

1 MONDAY
Moon Age Day 8   Moon Sign Virgo

The first day of June offers the chance to create a string of new social contacts and to make the most of all new opportunities that have been waiting in the wings. It isn't always the most obvious people who offer you the best incentives, and gains are possible from interaction even with individuals you have hardly noticed in the past.

2 TUESDAY
Moon Age Day 9   Moon Sign Libra

Talks with others should be informative and even enlightening, bearing in mind the present position of the Moon. There's nothing wrong with acting very much on impulse, and the more the year advances, the more perceptive you can become. Be prepared to include more people in your social life and to start exciting new activities around now.

3 WEDNESDAY
Moon Age Day 10   Moon Sign Libra

Look out for bonuses on the romantic scene and for the chance to really knock someone for six – just by being the sort of person you are! Your powers of attraction are emphasised, though you might sometimes be attracting people you don't really want around at all. Your strength lies in your ability to deal with difficult relatives.

4 THURSDAY
Moon Age Day 11   Moon Sign Scorpio

Trends suggest that at best there could be a competitive environment at home, and at worse everyone finds reasons to fall out with everyone else. Now is the time to play the honest broker and that means that you cannot afford to take on board anyone's specific point of view. Despite any frustrations now, you can still bring comedy into the mix.

5 FRIDAY
Moon Age Day 12   Moon Sign Scorpio

The planetary focus is now on your social life and mental interests. The most favourable developments at this time are related to money. Perhaps you have been able to gather a little more than you expected, or it could be that you are just making it go further. Beware of slight mishaps or silly accidents in sporting activities.

6 SATURDAY
Moon Age Day 13   Moon Sign Scorpio

A day of high energy is available, and with the Sun now so firmly in your solar fifth house you shouldn't have to look far for new incentives or the impetus to carry them off with aplomb. Even if the response you get from others is out of all proportion to what you feel you have done for them, why not allow them to be gracious if they wish?

7 SUNDAY
Moon Age Day 14   Moon Sign Sagittarius

Family matters continue to be highlighted, and this is a Sunday that can offer much in terms of contentment and happiness within the domestic fold. Don't get agitated about situations you can't control, and avoid getting stressed if things go wrong. Your best response is simply to smile at your apparent ineptitude and carry on just the same.

8 MONDAY
Moon Age Day 15   Moon Sign Sagittarius

You have what it takes to create a pleasant social atmosphere this week, and should welcome the chance to be at the very centre of anything that is going on around you. In terms of your personality, a cheerful approach works best, and assists you in your efforts to be the one who comes up with most of the good ideas at present.

9 TUESDAY
Moon Age Day 16   Moon Sign Capricorn

Look out for a little domestic friction. Mars is in your solar fourth house and that supports arguments with relatives or misunderstandings that aren't necessary if you pay attention to what people are actually saying. There are good reasons to give others a fair hearing at work too, because otherwise you could miss something of great significance.

10 WEDNESDAY   *Moon Age Day 17   Moon Sign Capricorn*

Trends encourage you to be alert, anxious to please and filled with the necessary enthusiasm to get things done. The only time you may become slightly frustrated is if, for one reason or another, you are not able to participate. Any unnecessary red tape could get on your nerves, particularly if you are determined to get the heart of things.

11 THURSDAY   *Moon Age Day 18   Moon Sign Capricorn*

With the Moon now in your twelfth house you can take advantage of one of the quieter days of the month. This doesn't mean you will be off colour or sulking. Rather, you have time to look at life from a slight distance and may well decide not to involve yourself in new projects today. This situation will soon change.

12 FRIDAY   *Moon Age Day 19   Moon Sign Aquarius*

Along comes the lunar high, a potentially smooth-running time when good interactions with those around you can lead to significant material gains. It should be easy to get others to do what you want, instead of having to follow pointless rules and regulations. A major success at work isn't out of the question at this time and could bring rewards.

13 SATURDAY   *Moon Age Day 20   Moon Sign Aquarius*

Make this your lucky day and capitalise on an excellent time for any sort of travel. Today isn't about being still for long periods of time, and activity is really important now if you want to make the lunar high work to your full advantage. Even if people generally want to have you around, bear in mind that you can't be everywhere at the same time.

14 SUNDAY   *Moon Age Day 21   Moon Sign Pisces*

Once again that position of Mars can get in the way of harmonious relationships at home. The secret is not to allow yourself to become involved in pointless discussions that could lead to arguments. Allowing others to believe what they want is fine, particularly if you feel that under present trends you can't alter their point of view.

15 MONDAY
Moon Age Day 22   Moon Sign Pisces

You can put your ingenuity to good use right now and steal a march on competitors as a result. Prepare to make the most of the chance to turn a profit of some sort quite quickly, and to pursue potential gains that are not of a financial nature at all. Love and affection always come easily to you, but are even more obvious at this time.

16 TUESDAY
Moon Age Day 23   Moon Sign Pisces

Quick thinking is worth a great deal today and should allow you to make progress regarding any issues that have been stuck fast for a while. Your intuitions are well accented, which is why you need to listen carefully to your inner voice. Even if friends are fairly demanding now, you can still enjoy their company.

17 WEDNESDAY
Moon Age Day 24   Moon Sign Aries

Right now you have a chance to display the charming, understanding and loving side of your personality. You can make romance in particular go with a swing and you could even turn the head of someone you have fancied for quite a while. When it comes to new activities, now is an ideal time to get involved and to remain focused on your objectives.

18 THURSDAY
Moon Age Day 25   Moon Sign Aries

The Sun remains in your solar fifth house, supporting a lively and energetic approach. Your romantic drives remain highlighted, and it will be possible for you to impress the people you see as being significant to your life. You can demonstrate a fun-loving attitude in most situations, and may also be able to boost your finances on the way.

19 FRIDAY
Moon Age Day 26   Moon Sign Taurus

The focus remains very much on your home life and particularly on the way you see things panning out for specific relatives. By all means offer all the help and encouragement you can, especially to younger people, though you need to bear in mind that there may be occasions when this is impossible, for reasons beyond your control.

20 SATURDAY   *Moon Age Day 27   Moon Sign Taurus*

Today would be a good time for getting together with someone special and for doing something that is miles away from your usual routines. Venus is now in your solar fourth house, strengthening even more that focus that presently falls on home and family. Of your love and affection there is no doubt, and showing it can make all the difference now.

21 SUNDAY   *Moon Age Day 28   Moon Sign Gemini*

There is much to be said for impressing those who admire you, and you can afford to take the trouble to do so today. It's also worth thinking about whether you have upset others in any way, as this in turn would probably upset you. Today is all about the way others see you, and whether you can change this.

22 MONDAY   *Moon Age Day 29   Moon Sign Gemini*

It looks as though you may be something of a perfectionist at the start of this particular working week and that's fine, just as long as you realise that everyone around you may not be. If you want things to go absolutely right, you may have to supervise them for yourself. The Sun now moves into your sixth house and that will certainly help.

23 TUESDAY   *Moon Age Day 0   Moon Sign Cancer*

A great deal could hang today on very specific decisions, most of which you will be making yourself. Although you needn't shy away from these, there could be occasions when it would be less worrying to hedge your bets. Your interests are best served by using an even split between common sense and intuition.

24 WEDNESDAY   *Moon Age Day 1   Moon Sign Cancer*

It looks as though the perfectionist within you is beginning to show again. You just can't stand things being done badly or especially downright wrong. What you need when the practical concerns of the day are out of the way is the chance to do whatever takes your fancy. With plenty of energy at your disposal, putting your feet up might not be your first option!

25 THURSDAY
Moon Age Day 2   Moon Sign Leo

The lunar low is around again and you can mitigate some of its worst qualities by simply pretending that it isn't there. True, you might decide to slow things down a little, but you have strong supporting planets and a great deal going on, especially at home. By all means let others take some of the strain – it doesn't mean you are incompetent.

26 FRIDAY
Moon Age Day 3   Moon Sign Leo

Dealings with authority figures could prove to be quite frustrating at the moment and it would be better not to get involved if you have any chance at all. Instead, why not please yourself and do only those things that take your fancy? If the attitude of friends seems strange, you need to ask yourself whether it is in fact you who are at odds with them.

27 SATURDAY
Moon Age Day 4   Moon Sign Virgo

A day to enjoy being involved in normal daily tasks, and now the lunar low is out of the way you have definite scope to make better progress. Confidence to do the right thing in affairs of the heart is well starred, and you can use it to make a good impression when it matters the most. The weekend has potential to be carefree and happy.

28 SUNDAY
Moon Age Day 5   Moon Sign Virgo

Unwanted issues can now be swept away, allowing you to concentrate on those matters that are closest to your heart. Today is about starting to define new goals for the future, and you might also be thinking about travel. Even little trips with those you care for would be beneficial, as would the chance to look at something very different.

29 MONDAY
Moon Age Day 6   Moon Sign Libra

This has potential to be a very busy day and one that may not always give you the chance to do what really seems important. Having to put things on the back burner constantly isn't an ideal situation. All the same, it is important to leave work alone once you come home and to turn your mind in alternative and fascinating directions.

30 TUESDAY

Moon Age Day 7   Moon Sign Libra

At this time it is important that you keep yourself in the right frame of mind to turn your attention towards possible success. Keep optimistic about your chances and don't automatically think you are incapable of doing something demanding. There is no limit to your capabilities – just as long as you really believe.

28

July

2009

1 WEDNESDAY
Moon Age Day 8   Moon Sign Libra

The spotlight is now on action you may need to take in order to improve conditions in your home and also possibly with regard to your health. Of course you might be worrying unnecessarily because that is part of the planetary indication at present. Maybe you need a total change from routines and the chance to do something just for fun.

2 THURSDAY
Moon Age Day 9   Moon Sign Scorpio

You now have what it takes to keep your interactions with those around you at home free from complications – a state of affairs that hasn't been the case for some weeks past. A great deal of good can come from spending time with people you see as being capable and inspirational, and you could even be indulging in a little hero worship now!

3 FRIDAY
Moon Age Day 10   Moon Sign Scorpio

New romantic interests could now be available for Aquarians who have been looking for love across the last few weeks or months. You are probably not one to settle for the first opportunity that comes your way, but now you have a solid chance to achieve renewed happiness. Be prepared to ignore the negative comments of others.

4 SATURDAY
Moon Age Day 11   Moon Sign Sagittarius

Tensions could arise if you find that your ideas are being thwarted or that others want you to follow their lead. You can now afford to demand to be heard and to have those around you admit that your way of doing things is best. The trouble may be that as far as someone else is concerned this genuinely isn't the case. Learn to relax if you can.

114

5 SUNDAY   *Moon Age Day 12   Moon Sign Sagittarius*

An ideal day to concentrate your energies on social matters and let all practical issues wait a while. Throwing in your lot with others works well, which is why team games and co-operative activities generally have much to offer you around now. Trends encourage your mind to wander, so that travel or even a contemplation of journeys is possible.

6 MONDAY   *Moon Age Day 13   Moon Sign Sagittarius*

This is definitely a time to exploit the best possibilities of your love life. Trends assist you to bring this into full bloom during the coming week, and you have everything you need to captivate that one, very special person. The depth of your affection knows no bounds, and you might even extend this to all those people you care about in a personal sense.

7 TUESDAY   *Moon Age Day 14   Moon Sign Capricorn*

A day to keep track of everything that is happening around you, and not to be tardy when it comes to making those important moves that allow you to stay ahead of the field. What matters the most is your ability to match practical skills to the level of popularity you can achieve at present. This combination helps you to keep succeeding.

8 WEDNESDAY   *Moon Age Day 15   Moon Sign Capricorn*

Conflicts could be the order of the day as far as your home life is concerned, which is why you may decide to commit yourself more fully to your work and to all practical matters. Even if you are not be the one who is creating difficulties, bear in mind that you may be the person who is expected to sort them out!

9 THURSDAY   *Moon Age Day 16   Moon Sign Aquarius*

The Moon returns to your sign of Aquarius and stacks almost everything in a way that looks good from your point of perspective. Despite the presence of the lunar high you will probably not be able to please all of the people all of the time. It's worth concentrating on those tasks you know are going to feather your nest in the weeks and months ahead.

10 FRIDAY
Moon Age Day 17   Moon Sign Aquarius

Current trends support a confident and optimistic outlook, assisting you to achieve a turning point in your fortunes. So strong is your personality at the moment that you can persuade others to accept in full your values and ideas and to be willing to do your bidding. Gaining the trust of colleagues in particular can really make the difference now.

11 SATURDAY
Moon Age Day 18   Moon Sign Aquarius

An ideal day to put extra effort into learning new skills, particularly at home, and to concentrate on achieving success when it comes to sorting out domestic details. Not that you necessarily have to stick around your own abode all the time. There is a definite drive to seek fresh fields and pastures new that remains with you all weekend.

12 SUNDAY
Moon Age Day 19   Moon Sign Pisces

Venus is now in your solar fifth house, assisting you to be kind, responsive and less inclined than has been the case recently to respond negatively to the moods of other people. On the contrary, it should now be you who defuses situations, and you can use your abilities to convince almost anyone that you know best. Few limitations need hold you back now.

13 MONDAY
Moon Age Day 20   Moon Sign Pisces

Where work issues are concerned, getting ahead at the moment has a great deal to do with being in the know. For this reason it is definitely worthwhile listening and watching even more than you normally might. Even the most casual remarks could have far-reaching implications and may assist you to formulate new strategies.

14 TUESDAY
Moon Age Day 21   Moon Sign Aries

Now is the time to gain from all kinds of input and information. However, you need to make sure that you are not simply gathering ideas together just for the sake of doing so. After preparation comes action, and you won't get any prizes for simply thinking what might work best. It is important at present to have the courage of your convictions.

15 WEDNESDAY   *Moon Age Day 22   Moon Sign Aries*

This would be a favourable time to sort out basic issues, to assess how things are likely to work out and then to do whatever is necessary to influence life in your favour. With a particularly good combination of intuition and common sense you have everything you need to be able to make definite progress. The planets offer strong practical assistance.

16 THURSDAY   *Moon Age Day 23   Moon Sign Taurus*

You tend to have a very unique style when it comes to living your life, and that is part of what makes you so popular with other people. Right now you should have your magnetism turned up to full, so that others won't find it easy to avoid or ignore your specific charms. Don't worry about being a little eccentric. That's another reason people like you!

17 FRIDAY   *Moon Age Day 24   Moon Sign Taurus*

Today you might need to avoid a slight tendency to be egocentric. Even if you feel you know best in a number of situations, it may not help your cause to tell everyone directly that this is the case. A little tact and diplomacy could go a long way and in the end will be what helps you to achieve such a strong competitive edge.

18 SATURDAY   *Moon Age Day 25   Moon Sign Taurus*

Capitalise on a socially uplifting time, both today and for several more days to come. What you learn when you are mixing with others could prove to be invaluable further down the line, and you should be more than willing to put in any amount of effort to ensure your popularity remains intact. Your love life can shine like a star this weekend.

19 SUNDAY   *Moon Age Day 26   Moon Sign Gemini*

The Sun remains for the moment in your solar sixth house and this strengthens your impulse to get things done during Sunday. There may be little inclination on your part to sit around and let others do whatever is necessary. On the contrary, trends support a burning desire to be involved in almost anything, and to be as helpful as possible.

20 MONDAY   *Moon Age Day 27   Moon Sign Gemini*

This is not the best time to be worrying about money or the general progress you are making in life. It would be far more satisfying under present trends to mix with others whenever you have a few moments to spare, and to keep yourself busy. Unnecessary worries are more likely to creep in on those occasions you sit around and ruminate.

21 TUESDAY   *Moon Age Day 28   Moon Sign Cancer*

An urge for a better and more fulfilling social life can encourage you to turn some situations around. Even if a part of your nature tells you that by having a good time you might be ignoring something important, this is far from being the truth. Mixing work and pleasure has never been easier, and enjoyment is the keyword no matter what you do.

22 WEDNESDAY   *Moon Age Day 0   Moon Sign Cancer*

Beware of getting so hooked up on the idea of making money that you forget what is really important in your life. It is love and affection that really count today, and you shouldn't have any trouble proving how much you care. There's nothing wrong with pursuing a lively social life, but it's worth remaining well in control of your emotions under all circumstances.

23 THURSDAY   *Moon Age Day 1   Moon Sign Leo*

The arrival of the lunar low indicates the possibility of minor problems at work. Instead of reacting adversely to these, your best response is to 'surf' life for a day or two. Now is the time to bob about on the ocean and keep your eyes open for the next roller. If you don't need to do anything much until the weekend, why not let others do it all instead?

24 FRIDAY   *Moon Age Day 2   Moon Sign Leo*

Your progress could well be sluggish at best, but you have the ability to improve matters if you encourage others to take on board more responsibility. You need to adopt a supervisory role and to offer the best instructions you can. Attention to detail could be slightly lacking, but most of the things that are necessary today rely on automatic pilot.

25 SATURDAY   *Moon Age Day 3   Moon Sign Virgo*

The Sun has now moved into your solar seventh house and what this brings is a greater potential for personal growth across the next month or so. A new friendship or love interest is more than possible, and this encourages you to put the best of what you are on display. If people love to have you around, you need to make the most of this.

26 SUNDAY   *Moon Age Day 4   Moon Sign Virgo*

This is a time of potentially wonderful events, some of which come like a bolt from the blue. Romance is high on the agenda, and Aquarians who have been looking for a new love should focus their efforts around now. New opportunities surround you on all sides, and even if you can't make your move yet, you can afford to do some serious planning.

27 MONDAY   *Moon Age Day 5   Moon Sign Libra*

Take advantage of all personal freedoms that you can create this week. Involving friends and colleagues in your pursuit of happiness can really make the difference now, and you can enjoy the affection they show in all sorts of ways. Keep abreast of local news and current affairs because you may be expected to participate at a moment's notice.

28 TUESDAY   *Moon Age Day 6   Moon Sign Libra*

Any slight pushiness on your part today is a signal that you want the very best for everyone. Of course people generally can't be expected to read your mind, so it is vitally important for you to explain yourself whenever the opportunity to do so arises. Not everyone will be impressed with you today, but don't be afraid to carry on anyway.

29 WEDNESDAY   *Moon Age Day 7   Moon Sign Scorpio*

You now have scope to be quite creative and very independent in your thinking. These traits assist you to mix with people who know their own minds as much as you do, though a few situations of conflict could emerge. Still, you don't have to agree with everyone in order to maintain your respect for them. Home-based matters are well starred.

30 THURSDAY
Moon Age Day 8   Moon Sign Scorpio

It is now towards your emotional and love life that your mind is encouraged to turn. You can make progress in relationships with others, particularly if you remain accommodating. If pointless rules and regulations get on your nerves, there is much to be said for ignoring at least some of them.

31 FRIDAY
Moon Age Day 9   Moon Sign Sagittarius

Socially speaking you may be something of a butterfly at the moment, with the ability to jump quickly from one situation to another in a totally seamless way. Keeping a dozen things in mind shouldn't be at all hard for you and there seems to be no lack of incentive when it comes to getting your own way or improving your lot.

28

August

2009

1 SATURDAY
Moon Age Day 10   Moon Sign Sagittarius

Communication increases with curiosity at the moment, and this is a trend that allows you to lighten your life no end. The weekend offers change and diversity, plus the chance to enjoy the summer weather and to get more fresh air. How about a picnic or a barbeque? As long as the company is good, it doesn't really matter what you decide to do.

2 SUNDAY
Moon Age Day 11   Moon Sign Sagittarius

Rather than making unnecessary assumptions today, your best approach is to rely on the evidence that stands before you. A cautious attitude works well in health matters, though worrying isn't the answer. Why not think about measures you can take to improve your physical condition before you start thinking you are ill? Aquarius often worries too much.

3 MONDAY
Moon Age Day 12   Moon Sign Capricorn

Work progress should come easier for you this week, particularly if you are determined to enjoy even those tasks that sometimes bore or trouble you. If other people seem to be taking a less than responsible attitude, this gives you a chance to show off how much more organised and capable you can be. Be ready to impress those in authority.

4 TUESDAY
Moon Age Day 13   Moon Sign Capricorn

Twosomes are where it's at for most Aquarians now. You have what it takes to enhance your life both at work and at home if you remain willing to co-operate. On the other hand, this doesn't mean you will be happy to do what others tell you. One option is to agree with what they say – and then do things in your own way!

5 WEDNESDAY   *Moon Age Day 14   Moon Sign Aquarius*

The Moon is back in your zodiac sign and the lunar high comes along at exactly the right time to encourage you to take a positive step forward. Take full advantage of your professional position and gain from things you are learning all the time. Your mind should be open to new input, and a focus on more practical matters is also emphasised.

6 THURSDAY   *Moon Age Day 15   Moon Sign Aquarius*

You have the opportunity to grasp new situations in a flash, and to impress others with the speed at which you learn and your mental capacity. There is a possibility that you are being watched, particularly by people who admire you and want to copy your techniques. It won't work for them, because nobody operates quite like an Aquarian in full flow.

7 FRIDAY   *Moon Age Day 16   Moon Sign Aquarius*

The potentially favourable interlude continues, and this would be an ideal time for anything that involves dealing with others. There are gains to be made from any such encounters, especially in a public forum, and this would also be the best period to take some time out and to do something completely new. Spur of the moment decisions are well marked.

8 SATURDAY   *Moon Age Day 17   Moon Sign Pisces*

Even if you prefer to keep a fairly low profile you can still remain in the public eye – that's one of the legacies of a seventh-house Sun. You have what it takes to dominate your surroundings, though you needn't do it in an aggressive way. Instead, it is persuading people to let you have your own way that counts for a great deal now.

9 SUNDAY   *Moon Age Day 18   Moon Sign Pisces*

Your ability to cultivate friendly relations with the world at large is part of what sets you apart for most of the time, but never more so than now. Now is the time to make sure that no one can find fault with either your methods or your suggestions. Affairs of the heart become more significant as the warmest month of the year assists you to heat things up!

10 MONDAY
Moon Age Day 19   Moon Sign Aries

This is a great time for all manner of informed discussions and for getting your point of view across to colleagues and bosses. Outside work a bright and lively approach works best, and enables you to make a favourable impression on the social scene. Don't be surprised if something completely new becomes a virtual obsession.

11 TUESDAY
Moon Age Day 20   Moon Sign Aries

Exciting things can be made to happen wherever you are now. Your strength lies in your ability to stimulate and enliven just about any sort of company, and these traits might be particularly useful if you are dealing with someone who is down in the dumps. You can afford to play the comedian for most of the time and to show off your sense of humour.

12 WEDNESDAY
Moon Age Day 21   Moon Sign Aries

Make the most of opportunities today to improve any relationship that has been going through a fairly low point. The sense of being at one with others can be quite wonderful, particularly if that's the way you prefer things to be all of the time. Don't be afraid to use new ideas to stimulate working hours.

13 THURSDAY
Moon Age Day 22   Moon Sign Taurus

Now you are encouraged to take a much more sensible approach to relationships of all kinds, and should be willing to put the more irrational and overemotional side of your nature on the back burner. The time is right to move your attention away from arguments and to concentrate on burying the hatchet in a very positive way.

14 FRIDAY
Moon Age Day 23   Moon Sign Taurus

A pleasant focus can be achieved at work and you have scope to get things to jog along nicely in a general sense. By all means do what you can to enjoy the season and get out into the fresh air whenever possible. You could vegetate if you stay in one place for too long, and in any case you can gain mental stimulation from any form of travel.

15 SATURDAY
Moon Age Day 24   Moon Sign Gemini

While the Sun remains in your solar seventh house, making progress in a personal and social sense is the name of the game. An ideal day for meeting new people and for finding stimulation and entertainment in new places. Today is not really about work of any sort, so you may decide that it's not worth pushing too hard towards objectives.

16 SUNDAY
Moon Age Day 25   Moon Sign Gemini

Beware of being a little precious about things today. There shouldn't be a problem if everything goes your way, though difficulties could arise if people throw obstacles in your path. Rather than arguing, discussion is the best way forward, and can help you to avoid any fallout later. Be prepared to welcome someone from the past back into your life.

17 MONDAY
Moon Age Day 26   Moon Sign Cancer

If you are pressing ahead with long-range ambitions, a serious rethink of past strategies would be no bad thing. Not everything you have done recently has been for the best, even though you may not have realised the fact until now. Why not get some sound advice from a friend and then start again? To do so is rarely difficult for adaptable Aquarius.

18 TUESDAY
Moon Age Day 27   Moon Sign Cancer

A day to capitalise on your penetrating insights, particularly in relation to specific issues that stand out in stark relief from the background of life generally. It's worth asking yourself how you could have been so out of step with others, and then doing what you can to alter things in a positive way. The Sun moving on in your solar chart supports these actions.

19 WEDNESDAY
Moon Age Day 28   Moon Sign Leo

Things could be rather tedious and trying today and you need to be as positive as possible in order to overcome the less helpful qualities of the lunar low. Remaining cheerful is the key, and as long as you ease off on the responsibilities it is possible that you won't even realise the lunar low is around.

20 THURSDAY
Moon Age Day 0   Moon Sign Leo

A time to keep your emotional demands to a minimum and avoid getting involved in heated discussions that could all too easily become arguments. To lose your temper might not be too much of an issue today, but there's a risk that you will end up feeling bad later and will have to do everything you can to put matters right. Precautions are better.

21 FRIDAY
Moon Age Day 1   Moon Sign Virgo

You have scope to show your caring and responsible side today, but you can also claim your share of the limelight. The best way forward is through co-operation, though trends also support a distinctly individualistic approach right now, encouraging a feeling on your part that your own ideas are the best ones to follow.

22 SATURDAY
Moon Age Day 2   Moon Sign Virgo

The Sun has now moved into your solar eighth house and that offers a month-long period that is filled with the chance to make changes. You may decide to take this opportunity to mull over relationships and consider how you can make them work out even better. Moving all the furniture around at home would be another option!

23 SUNDAY
Moon Age Day 3   Moon Sign Libra

Venus is now in a very good position to support romantic situations and new starts for some Aquarians. You can afford to look at life in a fairly positive way, though you might also be tempted to tamper with things to an extent that probably isn't wise. In a domestic sense, true happiness can be achieved by making everything conform to your expectations.

24 MONDAY
Moon Age Day 4   Moon Sign Libra

There isn't any doubt that you can presently emit an aura of power. If you ensure that others notice this, you can get them to follow your lead as a result. Social relationships are well starred, and new sights and experiences are the order of the day. What an excellent time this would be to take a holiday or to go off on a business trip.

25 TUESDAY · · · · · · · · · *Moon Age Day 5 · · Moon Sign Scorpio*

Professional commitments outweigh the importance of much else in your life for a day or two. Trends highlight your powers of concentration today, and you shouldn't be easily distracted – unless of course you are sitting all day by a window and staring out at the possibilities of the world. However, locking yourself in a box is probably not the answer!

26 WEDNESDAY · · · · · · · *Moon Age Day 6 · · Moon Sign Scorpio*

You run the risk of having authority figures working against you today, particularly if you become impatient when faced with pointless rules and regulations. Under such trends, this would be an ideal time to take action against something you don't agree with. One option would be to join some sort of pressure group.

27 THURSDAY · · · · · · · · *Moon Age Day 7 · · Moon Sign Scorpio*

You have great mental talent today for anything that demands greater concentration and an ability to see to the heart of situations. Be prepared to offer your advice to others, and to get them to follow your lead in various situations. Romance is possible for many Aquarians, and this influence increases as the weekend grows nearer.

28 FRIDAY · · · · · · · · · · *Moon Age Day 8 · · Moon Sign Sagittarius*

The Sun is now firmly in your solar eighth house, supporting a policy of 'off with the old and on with the new'. The spotlight is on how you deal with things that you see as being out of date or past their original importance. There is much to be said for tackling tasks one at a time. That's the best way of avoiding a terrible muddle!

29 SATURDAY · · · · · · · · *Moon Age Day 9 · · Moon Sign Sagittarius*

Looking and feeling your best can make all the difference at present, and you should have little trouble turning heads wherever you go. Venus brings out a special sense of harmony and also encourages you to make any necessary extra effort to show your affection. This is Aquarius at its best, and you can persuade the world to smile on you as a result.

30 SUNDAY   *Moon Age Day 10   Moon Sign Capricorn*

Be bolder and more adventurous and you can make the world your
oyster. Even if you have to commit yourself to work today, it's
worth spending as much time as possible in the company of people
who are simply good to have around. There are good reasons to get
to grips with finances later in the day.

31 MONDAY   *Moon Age Day 11   Moon Sign Capricorn*

The time is right for setting new objectives. You had a chance to do
this across the weekend in a personal sense, and now you have scope
to turn your attention towards work. You can afford to let certain
issues run their course and plan new adventures for the very near
future. Conforming to other people's expectations may not be
much fun today.

September

2009

(handwritten: 29)

1 TUESDAY

Moon Age Day 12   Moon Sign Capricorn

The first of September is a day for skipping along merrily and discovering your sense of uniqueness on the way. It's time to get a move on with plans that you know in your heart can't wait, and you should do better in almost anything if you are well prepared. Set your stall out carefully at work and be prepared to shine.

2 WEDNESDAY

Moon Age Day 13   Moon Sign Aquarius

Whatever you do at the moment will set the scene for the future. Even if it doesn't seem as though anything especially interesting is about to happen, you could end up being very surprised indeed. The Moon is in your sign and the lunar high offers new incentives, including financial ones. It's time to grab any bull by its horns.

3 THURSDAY

Moon Age Day 14   Moon Sign Aquarius

Taking the odd risk is what life is all about today. Even if these are carefully calculated, there is no point in following the line of least resistance under present trends. Don't be afraid to speak your mind, even though not everyone may be pleased, and make certain that the world knows you exist and that you intend to act.

4 FRIDAY

Moon Age Day 15   Moon Sign Pisces

Trends suggest that there is a good deal of hard work to be done, possibly without any immediate expectation of gain. You do have the advantage over other Air signs of being able to plan well ahead and past experience can also be a good guide at the moment. By all means structure your life well, but don't forget to let your originality show through.

5 SATURDAY   *Moon Age Day 16   Moon Sign Pisces*

This has potential to be quite a demanding day in one way or another. It's all very well deciding that the weekend should be put aside for enjoyment, but responsibilities have a habit of creeping in all the same. This shouldn't be a problem if you share tasks and have a laugh on the way. The focus is on your commitment to old friends at the moment.

6 SUNDAY   *Moon Age Day 17   Moon Sign Pisces*

A day to keep an eye out for snags in practical matters, and to think on your feet in order to avoid causing problems for later. Better by far to tackle something as a whole now, and to ensure that it is sorted once and for all. In a financial sense you need to find ways to enjoy the fruits of your past efforts much more.

7 MONDAY   ☿   *Moon Age Day 18   Moon Sign Aries*

You could spend so much time today trying to change things that you take on too much and exhaust yourself as a result. Rather than scattering your energies too much, why not try to concentrate on those matters you know to be the most important? When it comes to love, a more circumspect approach works best, together with a willingness to wait a while.

8 TUESDAY   ☿   *Moon Age Day 19   Moon Sign Aries*

If you have an ongoing relationship you can make the most of favourable events that have a bearing on both you and your partner. It's time to use the things that others do to give you a new outlook and a different way of viewing existing situations. Aquarius is gradually becoming a good deal more optimistic about many things.

9 WEDNESDAY   ☿   *Moon Age Day 20   Moon Sign Taurus*

You can now afford to put matters that you feel you have outgrown into the background, and the odd problem that has been around for a few weeks should also be less significant under present circumstances. By all means allow others to take a load off your shoulders, though bear in mind that this could leave you with rather mixed feelings.

10 THURSDAY ☿ *Moon Age Day 21 Moon Sign Taurus*

You may have to focus on tedious jobs today in addition to major goals and incentives. This could be the cause of a little frustration at a time when you really just want to get on as quickly as you can. There's much to be said for seeking advice from friends who you know will be warm and accommodating.

11 FRIDAY ☿ *Moon Age Day 22 Moon Sign Gemini*

Trends support a real need for excitement in your life at this time, and with the Moon now in your solar fifth house you have a chance to find new incentives to fill the void. Routines are best avoided if at all possible, particularly ones that generally bore you. Instead of doing things in your usual way, don't be afraid to look for an original approach.

12 SATURDAY ☿ *Moon Age Day 23 Moon Sign Gemini*

Today is all about your ability to get yourself into the good books of others, no matter what your association with them. There could be a new romance for some Aquarians or perhaps a change with regard to the way you see a present love affair. The weekend offers some exciting new possibilities that relate to money in some way.

13 SUNDAY ☿ *Moon Age Day 24 Moon Sign Cancer*

Prepare to bring some excitement to activities in general and to do all you can to enliven today. This is a Sunday for making choices and for seeing new places if at all possible. There are changes on offer as far as your home life or personal attachments are concerned, but you can make sure that these contribute to your happiness.

14 MONDAY ☿ *Moon Age Day 25 Moon Sign Cancer*

As the day advances, any uncertainty about specific aspects of your life probably has more to do with the approach of the lunar low than with any real problem you will be facing. Attitude is all-important under this trend, and you should be quite prepared to accept that some things will not be the same for a while.

15 TUESDAY ☿ *Moon Age Day 26   Moon Sign Leo*

It's possible that you could end up at cross-purposes with people who are genuinely trying to help you. Once again this is a reflection of the lunar low, which does little to assist your efforts to get on with others. Your best approach is to go with the flow for a few hours and avoid making unnecessary waves. An evening of relaxation would be no bad thing.

16 WEDNESDAY ☿ *Moon Age Day 27   Moon Sign Leo*

Slowly but surely you should begin to realise that specific aspects of your life are working out far better than you may have imagined. All the same, you might still be quite reluctant to give in to persuasion, and you can be really stubborn on occasions. As the day wears on, making sure you feel more like your old self is the name of the game.

17 THURSDAY ☿ *Moon Age Day 28   Moon Sign Virgo*

The Sun is still in your solar eighth house for the moment and this can sometimes bring what seems to be change for its own sake. Many of these alterations may be imposed upon you rather than being chosen by you. In a few days this trend starts to fade, so you can afford to be patient for just a while longer and to bide your time.

18 FRIDAY ☿ *Moon Age Day 29   Moon Sign Virgo*

Today is about capitalising on your good practical ideas, and the position of Mars in your solar chart assists you to take on the suggestions made by others. These can be incorporated into your own opinions and turned into concrete realities. In some cases you work best alone today, especially if something has to be done in a very specific way.

19 SATURDAY ☿ *Moon Age Day 0   Moon Sign Virgo*

If you are looking for a new partner, this could be one of the best times in the whole year to focus your attention on love. Venus is now in a favourable position as far as your attractiveness to others is concerned, and it is possible that some Aquarians will have far more attention than they really want! It's worth spending time with younger family members.

20 SUNDAY ☿ *Moon Age Day 1   Moon Sign Libra*

Travel and change are significant factors in your life at the moment, and some Aquarians could well be planning to go a long way very soon. The level of energy you have at your disposal is remarkable, a fact that shouldn't be lost on those around you. As a result you can attract a great deal of attention both now and tomorrow.

21 MONDAY ☿ *Moon Age Day 2   Moon Sign Libra*

A new understanding can now be cemented and a better atmosphere of tolerance is available for you now. There are quite big planetary changes in the offing, not least a new position for both the Sun and Venus. This can be an especially positive period for joint ventures, of either a social or a business nature. Money matters are well accented.

22 TUESDAY ☿ *Moon Age Day 3   Moon Sign Scorpio*

The workplace is a particular area of potential gain, especially if you remain professional in your approach to life. At the same time your patience is highlighted, and you can use your charm to make yourself irresistible to others and to increase your popularity no end. It isn't that you are different, more that you can get the world to notice you.

23 WEDNESDAY ☿ *Moon Age Day 4   Moon Sign Scorpio*

With a better approach you are now able to stabilise and to handle your relationships more positively than may have been the case across the last couple of weeks or more. If you can find out what people expect of you, that should make it easier for you to change slightly to accommodate their needs. All in all you can make this a very positive day.

24 THURSDAY ☿ *Moon Age Day 5   Moon Sign Sagittarius*

The focus is on broadening your social horizons at this time, and although the weekend is still a few days away there are good reasons to turn more towards social possibilities than to business matters. Caution is the key when dealing with sensitive issues, and your approach can make all the difference in terms of how your actions affect a friend.

25 FRIDAY ☿ *Moon Age Day 6   Moon Sign Sagittarius*

Intimacy is now important, and you can use this interlude to get much closer to someone you have always kept at a distance. It may not be that your attitude has changed that much, more that the people concerned are much more approachable. In most settings you can afford to show the warm, kind and diplomatic side of your nature.

26 SATURDAY ☿ *Moon Age Day 7   Moon Sign Capricorn*

Be prepared to take time out from the world and its concerns if you possibly can today. Unless you are definitely committed to work, there is scope for you to bring some enjoyment into your life and to ring the changes in a social sense. It's worth taking account of the dreamy side of your nature now, perhaps by taking short periods of inner reflection.

27 SUNDAY ☿ *Moon Age Day 8   Moon Sign Capricorn*

An ideal day to experiment and to work out how everything comes to be the way it is. Even if you welcome other people's opinions, in the end your strength lies in your willingness to try things out for yourself. Rather than getting bogged down with trivialities today, why not allow other people to deal with them? What you are looking for is interest.

28 MONDAY ☿ *Moon Age Day 9   Moon Sign Capricorn*

Prepare to pick up the pace again, as the start of a new working week offers all the promise of the approaching lunar high. You may not have a great deal of time for trivialities today and yet within some of them lie the germs of ideas that are coming along all the time. This is not a time to allow the grass to grow under your feet in any way at all.

29 TUESDAY ☿ *Moon Age Day 10   Moon Sign Aquarius*

The lunar high offers you the energy necessary to accomplish personal goals and ambitions. Today is a favourable time to consider where your professional life is heading, and for making the best impression possible on superiors. If you manage to get Lady Luck on your side, you can afford to throw caution to the wind – a little!

30 WEDNESDAY ☿ *Moon Age Day 11   Moon Sign Aquarius*

Improving your personal circumstances should be a natural aspect of life now, and there is plenty of incentive around to do so. The spotlight is on money matters, encouraging you to dream up new ways to firm up your financial position before the end of the year. Life is your best teacher today, so keep your eyes and ears fully open.

28

October
2009

1 THURSDAY
Moon Age Day 12   Moon Sign Pisces

With a new month comes the potential for a major monetary initiative, and this could prove quite important to your overall happiness. A practical matter may be easier to negotiate, particularly if you remain adaptable in your attitude and willing to learn new skills. What's more, you have what it takes to persuade others to school you if necessary.

2 FRIDAY
Moon Age Day 13   Moon Sign Pisces

This may turn out to be one of the busiest days for some time. Mars is in your solar sixth house, assisting you to define quite clearly what it is you want to achieve across the days, week and months ahead. What's more, you have what it takes to put new strategies into action and plough on regardless. A day to leave others breathless behind you!

3 SATURDAY
Moon Age Day 14   Moon Sign Pisces

You have scope to get more out of life in a general sense, although you could be on a bit of a downer when it comes to the way you view personal attachments. Perhaps this has to do with understandings that are taking place around now and it is definitely important to make sure you fully appreciate what others are saying – especially your lover.

4 SUNDAY
Moon Age Day 15   Moon Sign Aries

This month the focus is definitely on communication and that fact should be more than evident today. If you want to talk, you can find people around who are only too pleased to listen. Trends also support your efforts to complete a job that has been entertaining but difficult. New starts are there for the taking in the weeks that lie ahead.

5 MONDAY
Moon Age Day 16   Moon Sign Aries

Today could be a time of deep insights and you can use it to reach a situation in which life is laid out for you in a much clearer way than is sometimes the case. Helping loved ones in practical ways should be a natural aspect of life now, and this also extends to work, where your advice and your willingness to share effort can work wonders.

6 TUESDAY
Moon Age Day 17   Moon Sign Taurus

Professionally speaking there are signs that you could be somewhat overstretched now by an authority figure. At home your ability to get on well with others might not be quite as apparent today. Remember that if people are making demands on you that you can't accommodate, that could lead to a degree of awkwardness.

7 WEDNESDAY
Moon Age Day 18   Moon Sign Taurus

A phase of quite radical transformations is available. Mercury occupies your solar eighth house, giving you every opportunity to verbalise your ideas for change. Whether everyone will agree with you or not remains to be seen, but your powers of persuasion are well accented, and you won't need to feel frustrated.

8 THURSDAY
Moon Age Day 19   Moon Sign Gemini

There are good reasons to seek out the wide blue yonder, and a late holiday won't be out of the question for some Aquarians around this time. Even if you can't get away for a lengthy break, perhaps you could take a few hours out to do whatever takes your fancy. Ask yourself whether you are completely happy to do what others tell you.

9 FRIDAY
Moon Age Day 20   Moon Sign Gemini

Disagreements can still arise at work or in almost any situation where you have to follow the lead of people you either don't trust or see as idiots. A greater degree of co-operation would be no bad thing, though it may not be very easy right now to come to terms with certain individuals. Part of the trouble is that you are so original yourself!

10 SATURDAY
Moon Age Day 21   Moon Sign Gemini

A slightly greater sense of satisfaction can be achieved this weekend, assisted by the position of the Moon in your solar chart. For most Aquarians being away from work gives more space to see things in a clearer way, which is very useful. Rather than getting hung up on domestic chores, you can afford to take a break. What about a shopping spree?

11 SUNDAY
Moon Age Day 22   Moon Sign Cancer

It's great to travel, especially if you are an Aquarian. This is an ideal time to take off on a little adventure if you get the chance. You probably won't do yourself any good at all by sticking around at home all the time, and present planetary trends virtually demand a change of scenery. Intellectual pastimes are the most rewarding ones in which to indulge.

12 MONDAY
Moon Age Day 23   Moon Sign Cancer

The start of a new working week allows more scope for personal choice, even if you are still somewhat bogged down by a feeling that almost everything you do is dictated by someone else. Maybe you should ask yourself if you would do anything differently if the choices were entirely yours. It's worth keeping a sense of proportion today.

13 TUESDAY
Moon Age Day 24   Moon Sign Leo

The lunar low this month gives you an ideal opportunity to overcome difficulties and achieve your objectives. It's true that there are circumstances that might seem at first to hold you back, but you can make use of a strong determination and a sense of purpose. One thing at once is the best adage, so don't crowd your schedule too much.

14 WEDNESDAY
Moon Age Day 25   Moon Sign Leo

Feeling a little cut off from life in some ways is natural, but there is a great deal of personal choice about this, and you can take advantage of the chance to spend at least some time on your own. You need to think things through and that is difficult to do when you are surrounded by noise and activity. Make the best of a potentially pensive interlude.

15 THURSDAY　　　*Moon Age Day 26　　Moon Sign Virgo*

The Sun remains for the moment in your solar ninth house, which is where Mercury is as well. That allows a day of communication and a better sense of purpose when you ally yourself to others. Even if co-operation has been a problem of late, it should now be easier to see the other person's point of view. Be prepared to seek warmth from friends.

16 FRIDAY　　　*Moon Age Day 27　　Moon Sign Virgo*

The spotlight is on the Aquarius traits of being perpetually on the go and showing a positive hatred for any sort of routine you see as outmoded and boring. A day to use your natural sense of what looks right and to dress to impress if you get the chance. This can be especially important in professional settings or for social functions.

17 SATURDAY　　　*Moon Age Day 28　　Moon Sign Libra*

You work best when you are free to make your own decisions today – a trend that has been present for quite some time. It is probably too much to expect you to toe any line you don't care for, and some awkwardness is a distinct possibility if you discover that you have no choice in the matter. Try to stay cool, calm and collected as much as you can today.

18 SUNDAY　　　*Moon Age Day 0　　Moon Sign Libra*

Continue to broaden your horizons at every possible opportunity and do your best to impress people when you meet them for the first time. Even individuals who don't appear to have anything to do with your future success may be worth cultivating, because you never can tell. Be prepared to welcome new personalities into your life around now.

19 MONDAY　　　*Moon Age Day 1　　Moon Sign Scorpio*

Today you can afford to be very candid and determined to maintain control over your own life. It looks as though this is a reoccurring theme, though things could change significantly in only a few days. There are good reasons to continue to welcome newcomers into your social circle, because new friends can be made.

20 TUESDAY
Moon Age Day 2   Moon Sign Scorpio

Going after professional ambitions can assist you to achieve greater success now. The Sun is heading rapidly for your solar tenth house, which is going to be more useful to you in a practical sense. You are in a position to bring certain things to the boil, and to put in a little effort to make sure that life works out more or less exactly as you would wish.

21 WEDNESDAY
Moon Age Day 3   Moon Sign Sagittarius

Make the most of important news you can gather, some of which may come from surprising directions. There are pointers to your future if you watch what is happening in your vicinity, and no job should be beneath your dignity today if it gives you a chance to impress someone or achieve a desired objective. Aquarius can be positive again.

22 THURSDAY
Moon Age Day 4   Moon Sign Sagittarius

The restless side of your nature is to the fore, and you might soon get bored if you are expected to do things that go against the grain. Don't be afraid to get out there and do exactly what takes your personal fancy, though this might not be too easy just for the moment. When work is out of the way you should take the opportunity to shine.

23 FRIDAY
Moon Age Day 5   Moon Sign Sagittarius

Today you are best suited to a role that requires good leadership qualities and a positive frame of mind. You now have a chance to pick yourself up after a less than inspiring couple of weeks, though you can't expect everything to happen the way you want. However, you can take advantage of some positive surprises by the end of the day.

24 SATURDAY
Moon Age Day 6   Moon Sign Capricorn

Trends support a slightly provocative approach in personal relationships, though you can also attract others with your fascinating nature. Lively discussions are the order of the day, and with a number of different types of people. Avoid constant attention to detail at the moment because this could wear you out quite quickly.

25 SUNDAY   *Moon Age Day 7   Moon Sign Capricorn*

You can afford to show sympathy for the underdog today and to do all you can to help anyone who is having problems of one sort or another. By all means demonstrate your concern for those around you, though you need to ask yourself whether you might just be doing rather more than you reasonably should in at least one case.

26 MONDAY   *Moon Age Day 8   Moon Sign Aquarius*

Progress is there for the taking today. The lunar high assists you to be brighter, freer and more inclined to take chances. Any sluggish tendencies you experienced over the last couple of weeks can now be dispelled, allowing you to be on top form, especially in terms of your social and love life. Stand by to capitalise on some outrageous possibilities!

27 TUESDAY   *Moon Age Day 9   Moon Sign Aquarius*

The green light is now definitely on and you needn't let anything hold you back once you decide the time is right for action. A little positive thinking can go a very long way under present trends and you have what it takes to impress the most important people in your life. Love shines strongly in your direction, and you can reflect it wonderfully.

28 WEDNESDAY   *Moon Age Day 10   Moon Sign Aquarius*

Don't let yourself be restricted whilst Venus occupies your solar ninth house. For much of today the lunar high is still in operation, but there could be a slight feeling that someone or something wants to hold you back. It is crucially important that you take on board changes that you know are going to work to your advantage.

29 THURSDAY   *Moon Age Day 11   Moon Sign Pisces*

Social relationships may be a cause of some frustration now and you need to be right on form when it comes to the way you speak to people. This shouldn't be at all difficult for Aquarius, and you can be charm itself when you need to be. This is especially important if you are dealing with superiors or people with great influence.

30 FRIDAY
Moon Age Day 12   Moon Sign Pisces

Trends assist you to be at your most effective when it comes to practical matters, and there are definite gains to be made from alterations you make around your home. After a prolonged period when it seemed as if you were taking one step forward and two back, you should now be in a position to get most matters going the way you would wish.

31 SATURDAY
Moon Age Day 13   Moon Sign Aries

Be prepared to enjoy the thrill of travel and the chance to mix with those you find stimulating and even exciting. The Sun is now firmly in your solar tenth house, which is going to be of much more use to you and will offer new opportunities at every turn. An ideal day to put some effort into completing any outstanding jobs – particularly tedious ones!

29

November
2009

1 SUNDAY
Moon Age Day 14   Moon Sign Aries

You have scope to bring a more hurried feel to your everyday life and to make several things happen at the same time. Rather than getting hung up on details, the focus is on dealing with those matters that can be sorted out and finished in little or no time. Anything complicated should probably be left for another day.

2 MONDAY
Moon Age Day 15   Moon Sign Aries

Current influences support a strong desire for comfort and security. This is courtesy of the present position of the Moon and so it isn't a trend that will last more than a day or two. However, whilst it is around you would be wise to monitor your confidence levels and ensure that your responses to any threats are appropriate.

3 TUESDAY
Moon Age Day 16   Moon Sign Taurus

Even if you hate to be stuck in any sort of routine as a rule, this may not actually be the case under present trends. On the contrary, the focus is now on doing things in the same old way – a fact that might come as a surprise to some of your friends. Don't worry though, because even by tomorrow you can get yourself back to normal.

4 WEDNESDAY
Moon Age Day 17   Moon Sign Taurus

There are gains to be made by being very plain spoken in your dealings with others, especially at work. You needn't take no for an answer on those occasions when you are certain of your ground, and can be at your most dynamic in professional situations. At home a more relaxed approach works well, but you can still have very definite opinions.

5 THURSDAY
Moon Age Day 18   Moon Sign Gemini

A phase of strong personal magnetism is on offer, and today is a period during which it ought to be easy to influence other people to a much greater extent than of late. Be definite and determined and you shouldn't go far wrong. At this stage of the week slight concerns about money are a possibility, though you needn't allow these to last for long.

6 FRIDAY
Moon Age Day 19   Moon Sign Gemini

The curious and inquisitive side of your nature is highlighted whilst Venus remains in your solar ninth house. You can use this to find out how and why everything works the way it does, and especially so when it comes to relationships. Why not get tedious tasks out of the way early in the day? This will leave you more time later to indulge your curiosity.

7 SATURDAY
Moon Age Day 20   Moon Sign Cancer

Does it seem that there is no way of getting ahead today without doing what someone else wants you to do? This probably goes against the grain, but in the end you may decide it is necessary. Bear in mind that to refuse to take part would be to cut off your nose to spite your face. Of course you can be stubborn, but is that really your best option?

8 SUNDAY
Moon Age Day 21   Moon Sign Cancer

There are gains to be made today, simply by being in the right place to pick up on general good luck that is surrounding you. This is not a good time to sit around at home and vegetate. On the contrary, the more you interact with the world at large, the greater is the potential for gain. Socially speaking you have what it takes to be on good form.

9 MONDAY
Moon Age Day 22   Moon Sign Leo

Be prepared for your objectives to meet with a few obstacles today, and for the lunar low to slow things down somewhat. A philosophical approach works best if things do go slightly wrong, because what you are experiencing is nothing more than a short hiccup. You may feel happiest sticking to your normal routines.

143

10 TUESDAY
Moon Age Day 23   Moon Sign Leo

Even if circumstances seem to conspire to limit your horizons again, you needn't let this last for very long. There are some strong supporting planets around too and these begin to show themselves before the end of today. Capitalise on their influence by moving forward in romantic matters and by making favourable impressions on other people.

11 WEDNESDAY
Moon Age Day 24   Moon Sign Virgo

Now is the time to focus on career matters and to put as much energy as possible into getting ahead professionally. You have what it takes to excel at managing or supervising others, even if you have not been earmarked to do so. There is much to be said for showing yourself to be a natural leader at present, and for taking control when you can.

12 THURSDAY
Moon Age Day 25   Moon Sign Virgo

Your strength lies in your ability to make up your mind quickly about people, but there's a danger that you might take an instant dislike for no real reason. Giving people a little more time to make a more favourable impression would be no bad thing, because it is just possible that you are quite wrong about them.

13 FRIDAY
Moon Age Day 26   Moon Sign Libra

If you put yourself out you can be extremely persuasive today, and you can make some very definite progress without having to put in too much in the way of hard, physical work. Socially speaking you can be on top form and have what it takes to show yourself in a very favourable light when it matters the most.

14 SATURDAY
Moon Age Day 27   Moon Sign Libra

Prepare to make the most of all your professional options, even if you don't actually work at the weekend. If you are at work, then the trends are even better. Remember that people may be watching you closely, so it's up to you to display your best side. This means being efficient, friendly and ready to take almost anything in your stride.

144

15 SUNDAY *Moon Age Day 28   Moon Sign Scorpio*

It is towards the practical world that you can now look for some genuine support. If certain of your plans need slightly more than thought, you may have to put in some real effort to get over a particular hurdle. On the way you can find moments of real fun, most likely in the company of people you think of as being your best friends.

16 MONDAY *Moon Age Day 29   Moon Sign Scorpio*

Mars in your solar seventh house can leave you slightly susceptible to disagreements that are taking place in your vicinity. Your best response is to refuse to get involved, even if circumstances tend to draw you in. There are good reasons to physically isolate yourself from certain situations to avoid problems.

17 TUESDAY *Moon Age Day 0   Moon Sign Scorpio*

Your role in group activities seems to be highlighted now. Today is all about being optimistic, willing to fall in line with any reasonable request and flexible enough to change your direction at a moment's notice. By all means give yourself a pat on the back for a success you have achieved as a direct result of your hard work.

18 WEDNESDAY *Moon Age Day 1   Moon Sign Sagittarius*

You can combine your vigour now with a great deal of ambition and self-confidence. This could be one of the most favourable days of the month if you use it properly and there is little to stand in the way of material success. It is through careful, hard work that you can presently get ahead, and your superb concentration is what really counts.

19 THURSDAY *Moon Age Day 2   Moon Sign Sagittarius*

A little discontent is possible in personal attachments, even though this may be more or less forced upon you by circumstances. For this reason alone your   interests are best served by focusing less on romance and more on issues relating to the practical world. Once again the spotlight is on money matters.

20 FRIDAY
Moon Age Day 3   Moon Sign Capricorn

If you concentrate on making this a more comfortable and generally positive time, you can ensure that even the odd problem doesn't get you down much. On the contrary, you have what it takes to rise above difficulties and show everyone just how willing you are to join in and create fun. Anything you receive today counts for a great deal.

21 SATURDAY
Moon Age Day 4   Moon Sign Capricorn

Personality clashes are possible today. However, there's nothing wrong with refusing to join in, particularly as the Moon in your solar twelfth house assist you to be happier on your own. It isn't like Aquarius to crawl into its shell, but you may decide to do so before today is out. Staying focused on life generally is the best way to reap the rewards on offer.

22 SUNDAY
Moon Age Day 5   Moon Sign Capricorn

As today wears on so you can play a bigger and bigger part in anything that is happening in your vicinity. A timid approach would be no bad thing at first, but you can afford to turn this situation around once you get going. By this evening your interests are best served if you are willing to take the lead again.

23 MONDAY
Moon Age Day 6   Moon Sign Aquarius

The lunar high has potential to be a fantastic time for putting new plans into action. With everything to play for and a feeling of great confidence, you can now put the finishing touch to anything that has been waiting for quite a while. What is most noticeable about today is your ability to manipulate situations to suit your own needs.

24 TUESDAY
Moon Age Day 7   Moon Sign Aquarius

Remaining very much in charge is still the name of the game, but you needn't be selfish if you make sure everything you do is geared towards sharing the spoils of your successes. Romance is well starred at the moment, and where there was discord you can now sow harmony. Make full use of the level of popularity you have at your disposal.

25 WEDNESDAY
Moon Age Day 8   Moon Sign Pisces

Why not look to friends for both support and fulfilment? You are coming to the end of one particular phase in your life, whether you realise it or not, and new things need to be allowed in. There should be no problem with this as far as you are concerned, and you should be quite willing to wear almost any sort of clothes on your journey to better times.

26 THURSDAY
Moon Age Day 9   Moon Sign Pisces

In a material sense today offers you an opportunity to build successfully on past efforts. Anything odd or unusual could well grab your attention, and you can make gains from the strangest of situations. In particular, the emphasis is on making the most of any coincidences that you encounter around this time.

27 FRIDAY
Moon Age Day 10   Moon Sign Pisces

Mars, which is still in your solar seventh house, supports an element of annoyance today as a result of the actions of those around you. Prepare to think carefully about how you respond to the things that people say, rather than automatically getting on your high horse. Remaining cool, calm and collected is the key.

28 SATURDAY
Moon Age Day 11   Moon Sign Aries

Opportunities that present themselves today may not come again for quite a while, so there are good reasons to be fully focused on life. The need to pay attention assists you to concentrate on one thing at once – never an easy task for Aquarius. Don't be afraid to analyse your past efforts with a desire to improve.

29 SUNDAY
Moon Age Day 12   Moon Sign Aries

Bear in mind that those who have more power and control than you can be a source of support, and may even need advice in return. Gaining recognition for your knowledge and expertise is part of what today is about, and this also involves taking your responsibilities quite seriously. Family ties could be more important now than earlier in the month.

30 MONDAY
Moon Age Day 13   Moon Sign Taurus

You have scope to be much more dynamic and expressive today, assisted by the increasing power of the Sun in your solar eleventh house. Teamwork is important, as is the ability to share ideas with colleagues and friends. Their suggestions might even enable you to streamline your efforts and make greater progress.

28 ♒

December
2009

1 TUESDAY
Moon Age Day 14 Moon Sign Taurus

On the first day of December your task is to use the favourable influences in your career in order to start the month in a good way. You can afford to take a higher profile generally and will have what it takes to make an extremely good impression on other people. You might even be able to demonstrate your winning ways to those at a distance.

2 WEDNESDAY
Moon Age Day 15 Moon Sign Gemini

Romantic highlights should be prominent around this time, and even if the start of December is not the most memorable time in a personal sense, today at least should offer feelings of warmth and security. You shouldn't have to try very hard at all in order to get on the good side of others and this applies as much at work as it does socially.

3 THURSDAY
Moon Age Day 16 Moon Sign Gemini

Use your vitality, your natural sense of fun and your charm to increase your popularity with others. You may have to simply ignore anyone who doesn't care for you all that much, particularly if you are too busy to acknowledge them. This would be a great time to join new groups or clubs, but only after careful thought.

4 FRIDAY
Moon Age Day 17 Moon Sign Cancer

Positive highlights still come from being one of a group, rather than from going it alone. In any situation where you are one of a number of people involved in virtually anything, trends assist you to rise to the top of the pile and take charge. When it comes to your personal life you are now more inclined than ever to act on impulse.

5 SATURDAY
Moon Age Day 18   Moon Sign Cancer

What you are looking at now is great potential for personal growth. Lessons can be learned from situations that are terminating at the moment, or which have come to a logical pause. When you apply yourself to them again, or start something new, you should make sure you have gained a great deal in terms of experience and contentment.

6 SUNDAY
Moon Age Day 19   Moon Sign Leo

Be prepared to deal with a few unexpected responsibilities today, though these are situations you would normally take very much in your stride. It is probably only the arrival of the lunar low that makes things look more complicated than they actually are. If you break jobs down into their component parts you stand a better chance of getting them sorted.

7 MONDAY
Moon Age Day 20   Moon Sign Leo

The lunar low is usually a fairly heavy period and a time when you need to put in extra effort, but for today at least you have scope to create some surprising and happy scenarios. Even if you decide that some matters would be best postponed until tomorrow, your social life is well accented and you have a chance to achieve accolades at work.

8 TUESDAY
Moon Age Day 21   Moon Sign Virgo

Major irritations are a possibility, perhaps as a result of a failure to agree with what those around you are proposing at work. You may not have your usual patience, and it might take most of today for you to get back in tune with life. Once again it is your social life that could prove to be the saving grace. Here you will be charm itself.

9 WEDNESDAY
Moon Age Day 22   Moon Sign Virgo

The time is right to show greater sensitivity towards your friends and a willingness to listen to what superiors and people in general authority are saying. You might not be quite as radical as is sometimes the case, and may even epitomise the saying 'anything for a peaceful life'. Of course this probably won't last long because you are an Aquarian.

10 THURSDAY
Moon Age Day 23   Moon Sign Libra

Almost any sort of journey is well accented under present trends, and even though the year has nearly reached its end, a vacation of some sort isn't out of the question for at least some Aquarians around now. Even little outings to places of interest could help you to lift the gloom that can come with the approaching winter weather.

11 FRIDAY
Moon Age Day 24   Moon Sign Libra

Prepare to make progress in improvements at work and to capitalise on better fortune when it comes to money. It may only now have occurred to you that Christmas is just around the corner, and that could mean having to get your head round a great deal of shopping and lots of organisation. Even if you aren't ready, you can enjoy it all the same.

12 SATURDAY
Moon Age Day 25   Moon Sign Libra

You have scope to use your present friendly attitude to gain popularity with just about everyone and if there is a favour you need, now is the time to ask for it. There's nothing wrong with making reasonable requests, and in any case you have great persuasive skills. If you can get others to respect your opinion, this counts for a great deal now.

13 SUNDAY
Moon Age Day 26   Moon Sign Scorpio

When it comes to prior planning you have an opportunity to be at your best around now. Whether it's for Christmas or even for something further into the future, now is the time for some serious preparation. On the romantic front it you have what it takes to turn heads, and can use this interlude to get the response you need from your lover.

14 MONDAY
Moon Age Day 27   Moon Sign Scorpio

Relationships beyond your own front door could be slightly strained at the beginning of this week, particularly if you aren't able to get your own way regarding issues you see as being quite important. A day to avoid arguments and use your very good powers of communication to get your message across. Be prepared to remain patient with friends.

15 TUESDAY   *Moon Age Day 28*   *Moon Sign Sagittarius*

This could be a slightly strange and fairly unstable time in some respects. Mercury is in your solar twelfth house now, supporting a period of restlessness when you may be less inclined than usual to show your accustomed patience with others. There's nothing wrong with choosing to withdraw more than you usually would and to opt for peace and quiet.

16 WEDNESDAY   *Moon Age Day 0*   *Moon Sign Sagittarius*

Venus comes to the rescue today and offers a livelier social mood and the chance to return to winning ways at work. Rewards can be achieved through personal attachments and also through relationships that are taking a turn for the better. A closer understanding is possible with people who seem to have been distinctly awkward of late.

17 THURSDAY   *Moon Age Day 1*   *Moon Sign Capricorn*

Life can be a little like a seesaw at the moment because trends highlight both the sociable and withdrawn sides of your nature. Different aspects of your life engender alternative strategies, and today offers a potentially more contemplative day than yesterday. You can turn things in your direction much more next week, but for the moment, hang on!

18 FRIDAY   *Moon Age Day 2*   *Moon Sign Capricorn*

Any hasty actions at the moment could mean that you will have to think on your feet if you make unforced errors. In the end this may be no bad thing, because it does at least give you a chance to be out there batting for your side. Christmas approaches at breakneck speed, and it's worth being prepared to rearrange things at the last minute in a social sense.

19 SATURDAY   *Moon Age Day 3*   *Moon Sign Capricorn*

If today lacks any real excitement it does at least offer you the chance to take stock and also a few hours in which to get all the details right for whatever type of Christmas you are presently planning. If you haven't finalised things yet, it's worth finding time to do so now. In amongst all the practicality, there's nothing wrong with having some fun!

20 SUNDAY   *Moon Age Day 4   Moon Sign Aquarius*

The lunar high offers you the chance to make significant changes to
your environment. All your accustomed energy is at your disposal,
and the focus is on remaining cheerful and being willing to join in
with others. The Sun is approaching your solar twelfth house, so by
all means be thoughtful – but certainly not miserable.

21 MONDAY   *Moon Age Day 5   Moon Sign Aquarius*

Your personality now carries much more impact and there are gains
to be made from being in the right place to show how dynamic and
resourceful you are capable of being. The start of the last week
before the holidays ought to give you the chance to put something
into operation that will have a profound effect on next year.

22 TUESDAY   *Moon Age Day 6   Moon Sign Pisces*

Monetary opportunities are emphasised, and even if you are
spending quite freely at the moment there is much to be said for
keeping your finances stable. You can capitalise on your ingenious
thinking and should make the most of any small opportunity for
advancement that is available to you at this point in time.

23 WEDNESDAY   *Moon Age Day 7   Moon Sign Pisces*

With the Sun now in your solar twelfth house you are encouraged
to retreat somewhat into your own inner mind. The way this
displays itself at this time of year for you is generally through
nostalgia. You could well be looking back at Christmases from the
past and reflecting on how much life seems to have changed over
the years.

24 THURSDAY   *Moon Age Day 8   Moon Sign Pisces*

If you are not carefully organised you could miss your target as far
as a particular plan is concerned. Your best approach is to sort
yourself out as well as you can and be willing to seek the help and
advice of people who have very specific skills. Your ability to
entertain others can make all the difference in family situations.

25 FRIDAY
Moon Age Day 9   Moon Sign Aries

Trends assist you to ensure that Christmas Day is both happy and generally carefree, particularly if you can get others to contribute to a quite special sort of day. The focus is on actively seeking company, even certain people who are not generally involved in your merrymaking. You would be wise to avoid pointless disputes later in the day.

26 SATURDAY
Moon Age Day 10   Moon Sign Aries

There are signs that partnerships might not be working out as you would wish. The problem seems to be that you want to do one thing and they are set on another path entirely. Compromise is the key, and you needn't be afraid to be the one who makes the first more. Relax if you can and avoid getting steamed up over issues that don't matter at all.

27 SUNDAY
Moon Age Day 11   Moon Sign Taurus

It is possible that you may be slightly unrealistic today and that you could expect others to do more than they are willing to undertake. The focus is on getting your planning right in the first place and on not taking anything for granted. This is an ideal time to reflect on your life in a practical sense and to lay down plans for a slightly altered future.

28 MONDAY
Moon Age Day 12   Moon Sign Taurus

Venus is in the twelfth house of your solar chart, along with the Sun and Venus. This supports a reflective approach and even encourages you to withdraw from issues you don't care for the look of. As the year approaches its end you might be rather pessimistic about certain things, but in a practical sense you can show realism.

29 TUESDAY
Moon Age Day 13   Moon Sign Taurus

Any slight irritations that come along at the start of the day can be made to disappear like the morning mist as you bring your influence to bear on situations. It's up to you to respond quickly and positively, something that Aquarius can do easily. Friends may be warm and understanding, even if your life partner is not so accommodating.

30 WEDNESDAY *Moon Age Day 14   Moon Sign Gemini*

This may not be the best time to engage in strenuous activities, because you may be more susceptible to strains and sprains than would normally be the case. At the same time you may feel you have socialised enough to last half a lifetime, and there is much to be said for slowing things down socially. Why not try a new game or pastime today?

31 THURSDAY *Moon Age Day 15   Moon Sign Gemini*

The benevolent and understanding aspects of your nature are emphasised today, assisting you to gain popularity in most circles. Don't be surprised if New Year celebrations prompt mixed feelings. However, if you decide to get involved you have what it takes to be the life and soul of any occasion and to see in the New Year happily.

RISING SIGNS FOR AQUARIUS

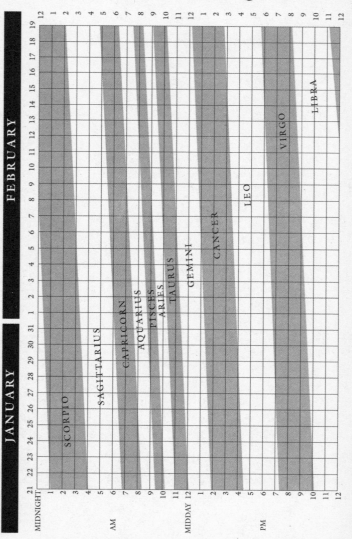

THE ZODIAC, PLANETS AND CORRESPONDENCES

The Earth revolves around the Sun once every calendar year, so when viewed from Earth the Sun appears in a different part of the sky as the year progresses. In astrology, these parts of the sky are divided into the signs of the zodiac and this means that the signs are organised in a circle. The circle begins with Aries and ends with Pisces.

Taking the zodiac sign as a starting point, astrologers then work with all the positions of planets, stars and many other factors to calculate horoscopes and birth charts and tell us what the stars have in store for us.

The table below shows the planets and Elements for each of the signs of the zodiac. Each sign belongs to one of the four Elements: Fire, Air, Earth or Water. Fire signs are creative and enthusiastic; Air signs are mentally active and thoughtful; Earth signs are constructive and practical; Water signs are emotional and have strong feelings.

It also shows the metals and gemstones associated with, or corresponding with, each sign. The correspondence is made when a metal or stone possesses properties that are held in common with a particular sign of the zodiac.

Finally, the table shows the opposite of each star sign – this is the opposite sign in the astrological circle.

Placed	Sign	Symbol	Element	Planet	Metal	Stone	Opposite
1	Aries	Ram	Fire	Mars	Iron	Bloodstone	Libra
2	Taurus	Bull	Earth	Venus	Copper	Sapphire	Scorpio
3	Gemini	Twins	Air	Mercury	Mercury	Tiger's Eye	Sagittarius
4	Cancer	Crab	Water	Moon	Silver	Pearl	Capricorn
5	Leo	Lion	Fire	Sun	Gold	Ruby	Aquarius
6	Virgo	Maiden	Earth	Mercury	Mercury	Sardonyx	Pisces
7	Libra	Scales	Air	Venus	Copper	Sapphire	Aries
8	Scorpio	Scorpion	Water	Pluto	Plutonium	Jasper	Taurus
9	Sagittarius	Archer	Fire	Jupiter	Tin	Topaz	Gemini
10	Capricorn	Goat	Earth	Saturn	Lead	Black Onyx	Cancer
11	Aquarius	Waterbearer	Air	Uranus	Uranium	Amethyst	Leo
12	Pisces	Fishes	Water	Neptune	Tin	Moonstone	Virgo